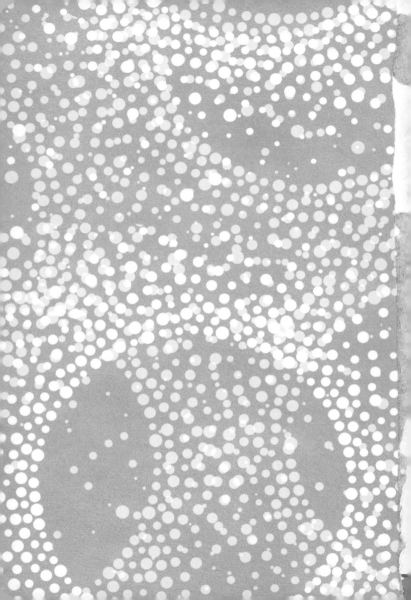

DETOX
FOR THE
SOUL

A 365-day
Devotional

BroadStreet
PUBLISHING

BroadStreet Publishing Group, LLC.
Savage, Minnesota, USA
Broadstreetpublishing.com

DETOX FOR THE SOUL

9781424566716
9781424566723 (eBook)

Devotional entries composed by Sara Perry.

Typesetting and design by Garborg Design Works | garborgdesign.com
Editorial services by Michelle Winger | literallyprecise.com

Printed in China.

23   24   25   26   27   28   29   7   6   5   4   3   2   1

Fix your thoughts on what is true, and honorable, and right, and pure, and lovely, and admirable. Think about things that are excellent and worthy of praise.

Philippians 4:8 NLT

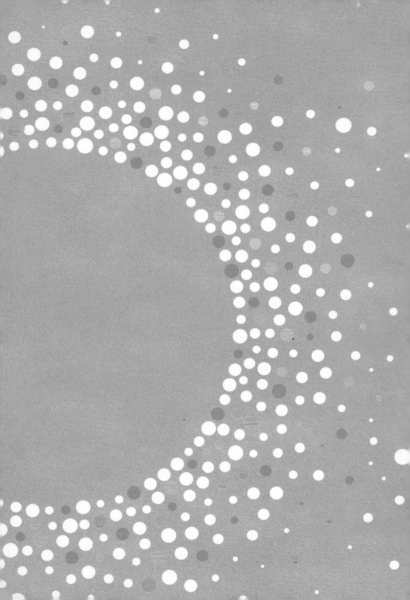

INTRODUCTION

It is all too easy to dwell on the negative aspects of life. We can talk for hours about conflict, worries, and disappointment, creating feelings of hopelessness, discouragement, and a lack of trust in our heavenly Father who is faithful, good, and just. Jesus said out of the overflow of the heart, the mouth speaks. What we focus on affects how we live.

This daily devotional will help you battle against toxic thinking. Renew your mind as you reflect on the Scriptures, devotional entries, and prayers written in this book. Identify your negative thoughts and compare them with truth. What does the Bible say? Are your thoughts honoring of yourself and others? Are they holy, excellent, or worthy of praise? Stop the downward spiral of doubt, comparison, and criticism, and choose instead to dwell on true, pure, noble, and lovely things. Enhance your mental, emotional, and physical wellbeing as you spend time in God's presence.

Detox your soul and experience the refreshing nature of a positive outlook.

JANUARY

Do not be conformed to this age, but be transformed by the renewing of your mind, so that you may discern what is the good, pleasing, and perfect will of God.

ROMANS 12:2 CSB

TRUE AND UNCHANGING

God, you are near me always, so close to me;
every one of your commands reveals truth.
I've known all along how true and unchanging
is every word you speak, established forever!

PSALM 119:151-152 TPT

Fix your thoughts on the nearness of God today. Make it a priority to bring your attention back to his presence throughout your day. As you do, reflect on the fruit of his presence in your life. Where is there love, joy, peace, kindness, and graciousness? Where is there room to both rest and grow in who you are?

The commands of the Lord are not meant to burden us but to liberate us. There is wisdom in the Word of the Lord. There is encouragement, direction, and acceptance. There is belonging, challenges, and an invitation to experience the steadfast mercy of God at every turn. Practice slowing down your responses when you feel yourself getting caught up in worry, irritation, or fear. Turn your attention to the nearness of your God and meditate on his faithfulness. He is forever good, and he is a ready help in every season of the soul.

Faithful One, thank you for being ever so near at all times. I lean on your faithfulness today. As I bring my attention and focus back to your presence throughout the day, release your peace, wisdom, and truth into my heart.

DELIGHTED IN

The LORD your God is in your midst,
a mighty one who will save;
he will rejoice over you with gladness;
he will quiet you by his love;
he will exult over you with loud singing.

ZEPHANIAH 3:17 ESV

If we are not proactive in our relationship with God, drawing near to his heart, we may miss out on the freedom of his love. God does not love us because he has to, but because he is compelled to. He delights over us with gladness. He rejoices over us with singing.

God's heart is tender toward us. It is to our detriment when we resist the graciousness of his affection. When we focus on the parts of us that feel "not enough" we allow the voice of shame to drown out the Father's delight. We are not accepted because of what we do, but because the Lord loves us as we are. His liberating mercy allows us to bloom in the light of his love. As we readily receive his delight as children of a good and attentive Father, we are free to live, move, and love others well.

Lord God, there is no one like you in love. You are pure hearted and true. I won't close my heart off from your love, especially the areas that need your mercy. Thank you, Father!

COMPLETELY LOVED

"The Father himself loves you."
JOHN 16:27 NIV

If we were to spend every day of our lives meditating on the truth that Jesus revealed in this verse, we would never reach the end of its impact. Love is the basis of the kingdom of God. It is who God is.

Instead of letting the idea of God's love become trite, let's press in to know God and his heart in a deeper way. The Holy Spirit reveals the wisdom of God, and we can trust him to show us new aspects of his love and how it plays out in our lives. As we are loved, so can we also love others. There isn't a part of us that is not reached or covered by the love of Christ. We are fully immersed in the mercy of God, and that is no small thing. It is the foundation of our faith, of our relationships, and of our identity.

Good Father, I admit that I need a fresh revelation of your love today. As I focus on your love, reveal what I could not perceive before. I want to know the power, the length, and the breadth of your mercy-kindness. Open my eyes even as I feel your love expand my heart.

HIGHER PERSPECTIVE

Raise your eyes on high
and see who has created these stars,
the One who brings out their multitude by number,
he calls them all by name;
because of the greatness of his might
and the strength of his power,
not one of them is missing.

ISAIAH 40:26 NASB

When life is overwhelming, it can feel as if the walls of this world are closing in on us. This is the perfect time to expand our perspective, and there are practical ways we can ground our bodies, minds, and hearts in this way.

Take today's verse, for instance. When we physically stand in a space that reminds us of our smallness, it can bring great comfort to know that God is much larger than we can imagine, and so is his wisdom. Whether you go to the ocean and stare over the great waters, stand under the dark sky and look up into the heavens and see the twinkling of stars, or hike a mountain to gain higher perspective, take some time to physically get into a space that reminds you of the Creator and his vast power. As you do, remind yourself that even the great trials of your life do not overwhelm your God.

Creator, thank you for the cues of your greatness in creation. As I step outside and consider your handiwork, bring rest, peace, and perspective to my heart and life.

SUREFOOTED AND STRONG

The Sovereign LORD is my strength!
He makes me as surefooted as a deer,
able to tread upon the heights.

HABAKKUK 3:19 NLT

When we are overtired and worn-down, it can be difficult to focus on anything else. Yet, the Scriptures say over and over again that the Lord is our strength. In our weakness, he makes us strong. When we run out of our own vigor, we lean on him, and he carries us. He steadies our feet in troubled times.

It is good to recognize our limits. When we are weary, we should rest. When we are hungry, we should eat. God does not want us to neglect ourselves so that we burnout. Rest is holy. Still, there are things that we cannot rest ourselves out of. In times and seasons when life keeps going and we have little to give on our own, the Lord offers us his own grace-strength. Let's look to him in our times of need, for he is faithful to offer all that he has and is to us. What a glorious hope!

Lord, make my feet sure and my resolve strong. When I have nothing more of my own to give, you always have an abundance of what I need: peace, joy, strength, hope, and love. Fill me afresh today.

GOOD NEWS

"The LORD, the LORD is a compassionate and gracious God,
slow to anger and abounding in faithful love and truth."
EXODUS 34:6 CSB

Where we can be quick to judge, God is thoughtful and
gracious. He sees what we cannot—the full picture, as well as
the intentions of every heart. The Lord is not quick to silence
us when we assert our needs. He is kind, merciful, and
abounding in faithfulness.

When you feel yourself jumping to conclusions about others
and their motives today, bring it under the canopy of God's
grace. It is not your job to judge others, but to love them.
And what does God's love look like? It is slow to anger,
abounding in grace and kindness. May you find yourself
enveloped in the mercy of God today, and from that place
give out of the abundance of his pure love to others.

Gracious God, you see my heart in all of its stages. You are
so much better than this world that pins people down with
judgment. You are so merciful and gracious, slow to anger
and abounding in love. I want to reflect you in the way I
move in this world. Help me, Lord.

SO MUCH MORE

With God's power working in us, God can do much,
much more than anything we can ask or imagine.

EPHESIANS 3:20 NCV

If we put our minds to something, it is very likely that we
can accomplish it. There is value in hard work and focus.
Even so, there are limits to our abilities, and we cannot
account for unforeseen obstacles in life. We cannot control
what the world will do, accidents that will happen, or how
loss will affect us. When our plans go off-track, we are not
without hope. God is faithful, and his mercy will hold us
together in ways we could never have anticipated.

God is able to do immeasurably more than anything we
can imagine or ask him to do. His power is fueled by love, it
doesn't miss a detail, and it can resurrect and redeem what
we could not on our own. His ways are better, his thoughts
are better, and his intentions are better for us than we have
for ourselves. Let's trust him to do what only he can do, even
as we ask him to intervene in our lives.

Mighty God, I know that you are able to do more than I
can even venture to imagine. Even so, I will stretch my
imagination to partner with your love and power. Have your
way in my life. I trust you.

GIVE THANKS

Oh, give thanks to the LORD!
Call upon His name;
Make known His deeds among the peoples!
1 CHRONICLES 16:8 NKJV

The practice of gratitude is a powerful tool in directing our attention to the good things of this life—the good gifts God has given us. We don't have to ignore our needs or the very real pressures we are under. We can bring those to God in prayer, knowing he hears us. But let's not stop there.

Today, take the time to make a gratitude list. What are the things you are thankful for? Who are the people in your life that you are grateful for? Nothing is too small if it brings you comfort and joy. As you go about your day, make note of the things that offer peace, joy, hope, and love. Thank God for every one and consider sharing some of the practical acts of his goodness in your life with others.

Lord, thank you for this day—for another opportunity to be known, to create, to live, move, and have my being. I am so grateful for the gifts of this life. Be honored as I pour out my gratitude to you every time I recognize your blessing in my life.

A COMPELLING FOCUS

I don't depend on my own strength to accomplish this;
however I do have one compelling focus: I forget all of the
past as I fasten my heart to the future instead.
PHILIPPIANS 3:13 TPT

Ruminating on the past can make us feel stuck in the
present. When shame comes knocking on the doors of
our hearts as we see things we could have done differently,
it is important that we invite Christ's perspective over us.
We have to let go of what was in order to move ahead. We
cannot hold ourselves in the prison of perfectionism and
expect to thrive.

Instead of dwelling on things that we cannot change in the
past, we can shift our focus to who God is, who he says
we are, and what he has for us in the future. As we ground
ourselves in the overwhelming love of Christ that meets
us in the right here and now, we can move forward with
confidence. Christ is our compelling focus.

Lord Jesus, I let go of the shame that made me feel stuck and
I receive your love that lifts me out of that pit. I choose to
follow you, eyes fixed on who you are. Thank you for loving
me, redeeming me and calling me yours.

NO SHAME

Hope does not put us to shame, because God's love has been poured into our hearts through the Holy Spirit who has been given to us.

ROMANS 5:5 ESV

Hope does not put us to shame. What a powerful statement. The Holy Spirit does not work within our hearts to produce shame, but to shower us in love. We come alive in the truth of Love's light. We have been given grace upon grace.

Even in times of trouble, as Paul says in Romans 5:3, we have a joyful confidence in Christ. As we endure, our character is strengthened and refined, and that leads us back to our shame-free hope. If you are struggling against condemnation because you are going through a tough time, be sure of this: that is not from God. He who calls you his own reaches out in tender mercy, gracious strength, and astounding peace. Rise up in the confidence of who Christ says you are and throw off the shackles of shame. You don't have to live under condemnation's abuse any longer. You are free in Christ, and he is your living hope.

Holy Spirit, flood my senses with the power of your love until I am filled with the sense of expansive belonging, empowered determination, and peaceful resolution. You are my hope.

UNDER LOVE'S BANNER

He has brought me to his banquet hall,
and his banner over me is love.
SONG OF SOLOMON 2:4 NASB

When we live under the banner of God's love, no arrows of accusation can rip us apart. When we become aware of areas in our lives that aren't in alignment with the good news of Christ, we have the opportunity to repent and repair. Love doesn't excuse our mistakes, but it also doesn't hold them against us.

The Scriptures declare that the mercies of God are new every morning. There is a fresh portion of compassionate mercy in every moment. When we turn to God, we find ourselves enveloped in his love, completely covered by the banner of his affection. It is greater than any fear, shame, or regret. What an invitation we have today: to rejoice in the faithfulness of God's great love that covers us.

Merciful God, thank you for the power of your persistent love. I yield to your mercy, for it is my strength, my joy, and my peace. Wherever I am out of alignment with your heart, bring me into position today. I am yours, and I surrender to your ways.

TRANSFORMED MINDSETS

Don't copy the behavior and customs of this world, but let God transform you into a new person by changing the way you think. Then you will learn to know God's will for you, which is good and pleasing and perfect.

ROMANS 12:2 NLT

The way we think informs the way we live. If we are full of fear, skepticism, and anger, then the paths we choose will show it. The fruit of our lives reflects what we take in. Our motivations matter, but so do the wells we draw from.

Take some time with the Lord in prayer and ask the Holy Spirit to reveal mindsets that don't reflect his kingdom. Don't copy the behavior of others around you simply because they are customary. Let God speak his higher perspective, his life-giving wisdom, and allow yourself to be transformed as you do what he shows you to do. Where there is love, peace, joy, patience, kindness, along with all the fruit of God's Spirit, there is a trustworthy source to draw from.

Spirit, transform my thoughts, down to the way I think about things, in your gracious presence. I don't want to fall in line with tradition and others' expectations; I want to reflect you from the inside out in every part of my life.

CREATIVELY PUT TOGETHER

You created my inmost being;
you knit me together in my mother's womb.
I praise you because I am fearfully and wonderfully made;
your works are wonderful,
I know that full well.
PSALM 139:13-14 NIV

When we find our worth in what others think of us, it is as if we are trying to hit a moving target. Beauty standards change all the time, as do fashions. What once was sought becomes yesterday's news as trends move.

What would it look like for you to accept yourself for who God created you to be? You don't have to change a single thing to find yourself fully loved and accepted by your Father in heaven. The things you see as quirks are creative inputs of an attentive Creator. You are fearfully and wonderfully made—you. Just as you are. When you are tempted to cover your perceived flaws, offer loving acceptance. Make it a practice and see how it changes the way you see yourself. You are worthy of love, you fearfully and wonderfully made image of the divine.

Creator, I want to love myself the way that you love me—completely. Help me to grow in compassion toward myself, as well as grounded identity in who you have wonderfully created me to be.

WHAT A SAVIOR

"Let us praise the LORD, the God of Israel,
because he has come to help his people
and has given them freedom.
He has given us a powerful Savior."

LUKE 1:68-69 NCV

God did not leave us without help in this world. He sent his Son, Jesus Christ, to help us and to liberate us. No matter what hard times we go through, we are free from the curse of sin, fear, and death. We are liberated in Christ here and now, not only in the kingdom to come.

This is extraordinarily good news. No one can take away the power of love that saves us. We can turn our attention to the very near presence of God and to the hope of our hearts, Jesus Christ. Even when pressure rises, God's peace is ever so near. Let's lean into it, fixing our eyes on our wonderful Savior. As we do, we will know the freedom of his love, peace, and joy in even greater measures.

Savior, thank you for the freedom I find in you. Continue to peel back the layers of my heart as I put all my trust in you.

NO MORE STRIVING

"Don't strive for what you should eat
and what you should drink,
and don't be anxious."
LUKE 12:29 CSB

Worrying and striving deplete our emotional energy. Jesus instructed his followers to give up striving for the necessities and to lay aside their worries. In fact, he invited them to leave their worries with him.

When we cannot avoid the anxiety that crops up and the fear that pushes us to strive for things rather than rest in trust, we don't have to simply ignore the feelings. That won't do anything to help us, for it won't go anywhere at all. Let's take every worry and anxious thought and bring it to Christ, and let's leave them there with him. He can be trusted, and he offers us peace in their place.

Trustworthy Savior, I don't want to keep toiling for what you offer me for free. Rather than striving for the bare minimum, I trust you to provide, and I partner with your heart and rest in your peace.

NEVER TOO FAR GONE

"The Son of Man has come to seek and to save
that which was lost."
LUKE 19:10 NKJV

It is never too late to choose to do better. You are not too far-gone, no matter what mess you may find yourself in. The grace and mercy of Jesus Christ is powerful to save, and he came to seek and to save that which was lost.

When you are tempted to give into despair, instead invite Christ into the home of your heart. Allow him to enter your life, to rearrange what needs to be shifted and to receive the gracious restoration of his love. He can do far more than you can imagine. Simply humble yourself, welcome him in, and allow him to do what he will do in you. His love is better than your shame, guilt, or fear. It is more powerful than any threat or trouble you are in. Trust him, for he is good, and he is able to save you.

Jesus Christ, in you I put my hope—even the last dregs of it. I don't want to waste away in despair. Come into my heart and life today and bring restoration, redemption, and life. I yield to you, for you are my Savior.

FASTEN YOUR FAITH

It is through him that you now believe in God, who raised
him from the dead and glorified him, so that you would
fasten your faith and hope in God alone.

1 PETER 1:21 TPT

Consider today what your hopes are fixed on. Is it the next
promotion, an overhaul of your finances, or a relationship that
you feel could fix everything that feels out of order in your
life? It doesn't take long to realize that once we receive what
we had long awaited, our hopes latch onto the next thing.

Christ is the source of every longing, desire, and need. He is
the well we draw from to find our satisfaction. His presence
brings perfect peace, jubilant joy, and overwhelming hope.
His lavish love both expands our expectations and fulfills
them. Instead of looking for satisfaction outside of ourselves,
let's look to the one who chooses to dwell within through his
Spirit. As we fasten our faith and hope to him, he releases
more of himself over us. He is worthy of our trust, our
devotion, and our attention—now and always.

Faithful One, I choose to look to you today for all that I
need. I bring you my unfulfilled longings and ask for your
presence to fill me up with the wonderful goodness of your
living love. I fasten my faith to you.

PERMISSION TO CHANGE

When I was a child, I talked like a child, I thought like
a child, I reasoned like a child. When I became a man,
I put the ways of childhood behind me.

1 CORINTHIANS 13:11 NIV

Just as we go through developmental stages in our bodies,
cognition, and emotions, we also go through faith stages.
Growth in faith looks like maturity. Though children see the
world as black and white, fact or fiction, adults are able to
see the gray between, the nuances of life. We cannot expect
our spiritual lives to remain the same throughout our lives;
no more than we could expect a child to remain small and
within the limitations of their young selves.

It is healthy to embrace the changes that you have experienced.
You are always learning and growing, even until the day you
die. As you discover there is less you can control than you once
thought, allow yourself to let go of the need and surrender
to the mystery. God is still with you. He is still guiding you.
He is true, and he never changes. It is right to change your
mind about things when you have a better picture and more
information. Allow yourself to do it; it is not a threat to your
faith, but rather necessary to its growth.

Father, thank you for the chance to change, mature, and
grow. I embrace it.

PARTNER WITH HIM

"Be strong and courageous, and do the work. Don't be afraid or discouraged, for the LORD God, my God, is with you. He will not fail you or forsake you. He will see to it that all the work related to the Temple of the LORD is finished."

1 CHRONICLES 28:20 NLT

Having faith in God does not mean that we sit back and wait for him to move on our behalf in every season of our lives. There is power in our partnership. Be strong and courageous, and do the work. What is "the work" that you know to do? It really is simple. Put your faith in God, and do what is yours to do.

Instead of getting lost in the what ifs today, take hold of what you know to be true. Even if the work looks like feeding your family today, it is not without value. You are a builder in the kingdom of your Father, and your efforts to partner with his purposes have lasting effect. Don't neglect your part, for your role is unique and imperative. In all things, do it with love, and it will not be wasted.

Lord, help me to focus on your help and the work that is mine to do. I don't want to get caught up in what isn't being done by others. You are my strength and courage, and I choose to partner with you.

ALWAYS THE SAME

Jesus Christ is the same
yesterday and today and forever.
HEBREWS 13:8 NASB

In a world full of constant change, there is one who remains the same forever. He is forever moved with compassion, full of marvelous mercy, and overflowing with kindness. He is just, true, and always sees things clearly.

When we feel overwhelmed by the unknowns of tomorrow, we can take refuge in the constancy of our Lord God. He is a safe place to find shelter. He sees the end from the beginning, and everything between, and he is full of wisdom, strategy, and power. He can restore even what feels irredeemable. He is better than the best of us. Let's throw the anchor of our hope into the abundant waters of his strong love, for they will never run dry.

Unchanging One, as I meditate on your goodness and your grandeur, I cannot help but be filled with the peace of your presence. You are trustworthy and true, and you will never change. You are not vengeful or controlling. You are generous and kind, and how I love you for it. Transform my heart in the power of your nature.

WORDS TO LIVE BY

"Render true judgments, show kindness and mercy to
one another, do not oppress the widow, the fatherless, the
sojourner, or the poor, and let none of you devise evil against
another in your heart."

ZECHARIAH 7:8-10 ESV

Love is liberating, not controlling. It is full of kindness and
grace. It is not biased, nor is it manipulative. The law of
love reigns over every tradition, regulation, and law of this
world. We are not to act as the world does, but we are to be
extravagant in loving-kindness, generous with what we have,
and compassionate with others.

We should do better because we have received from the
overwhelming abundance of God's love. We should be light
to the world, spreading mercy and caring for the vulnerable.
Instead of drawing lines in the sand, we should be tearing
down walls and building bridges. This is the way of Christ's
kingdom.

Lord, when I consider how you instruct us to live and how
I actually treat others, I see so much room for growth in
myself. Help me to put away the old ways of treating others
how I am treated and turn the tables. May I follow your path
of love, even and especially when it feels hard to do so. I
believe that it is worth it.

OPEN THE DOOR

"See! I stand at the door and knock.
If anyone hears my voice and opens the door,
I will come in to him and eat with him, and he with me."

REVELATION 3:20 CSB

Jesus stands at the door of your heart, knocking. Do you hear his voice? Open the door to him, and welcome him in. There is unbroken fellowship in his presence, and there we find abundantly more than all that we need. He is good, and he loves us to life over and over again.

We could remain closed off to the ways of Christ, or we can embrace his paths of peace. It all starts in our hearts, in union with his Spirit. Even if all you can do is crack the door of your heart open a little to peek out, he is standing there ready to reveal his goodness to you. He is kind, and his kindness leads to repentance. He is not full of anger toward you for all of your failures but of love to restore you. Will you open up to him today?

Jesus Christ, I don't want to struggle on my own any longer. Even when I feel resistance, I will open the door to you. Reveal the truth of your love to me as I do. I want to be washed in the refreshing waters of your love and restored in your mercy.

AUDIENCE OF ONE

"Pray to your Father, who cannot be seen.
Your Father can see what is done in secret,
and he will reward you."
MATTHEW 6:6 NCV

When we work for the attention and affirmation of others,
we become like hamsters on a wheel, spinning and spinning
but going nowhere. Instead of putting our energy into others'
perceptions of us, let's follow our hearts and do what is right
and good for the audience of our Father. He sees what no
one else does, and he will never overlook our efforts of love.

Every sacrifice and surrender is accounted for. Every
movement of mercy is noted. As we dedicate our days to
him, we can be sure that even the smallest choices have
larger effects. Integrity keeps us honest when no one else is
looking, for we know that God always is. We don't have to
publish our good deeds, but we can be sure that God notices
each and every one.

Father, I know that you see what others miss. I don't want to
strive for attention or affirmation from others. I want all I do
to be rooted from a place of love and confidence in knowing
that it matters to you. Thank you for not missing a thing.

THERE IS HOPE

There is hope for a tree, if it is cut down,
that it will sprout again,
and that its tender shoots will not cease.

JOB 14:7 NKJV

When we go through hard times, our lives becoming smaller than we imagined they would, God is still faithful. There is always hope. As long as we are living, there is redemption, restoration, and mercy. Even if a tree is cut down, there is hope for it to sprout again. Do we believe the same can be true for us?

No matter what setbacks you face, you can trust that there is hope for redemption. There is new life that can sprout from the ashes of what has burned to the ground. Once you are through the painful grief, know that the cleansing power of a fresh start is beautiful ground for hope. Your hopes are not in vain, for if they are rooted in the Lord, they will be nourished and produce fruit. Dare to hope today, even in the face of loss.

Restorer, thank you for the hope that does not fail. I trust that you are not finished with me yet. Have your way in my life and bring new life out of the ashes of despair. I am rooted in you.

OUT FROM FEAR

God will never give you the spirit of fear, but the Holy Spirit who gives you mighty power, love, and self-control.
2 TIMOTHY 1:7 TPT

Though many systems and people of this world lead with fear, God does not. He does not seek to control us through fear, nor does he hold us captive by it. He liberates us with love every single time. Where there is fear in our lives, it is certainly not the work of God.

The Holy Spirit gives us mighty power, love, and self-control. Self-control is an ability to tell the difference between what is tempting and what is good for us and to choose the better thing. We are not slaves to our desires or to the pull of the world. We are free to choose and to choose well because the Spirit of God is alive in us. Let's come out from under fear's restrictive hold on our lives and walk in the power, love, and self-control of the Spirit.

Great God, I will not fear what others may say or do against me. I choose to live in the liberation of your love and follow the wisdom of your truth. Your ways are so much better than the ways of this world.

TRUST HIM

Nothing in all creation is hidden from God's sight.
Everything is uncovered and laid bare before the eyes of him
to whom we must give account.

HEBREWS 4:13 NIV

It is exceedingly good news that nothing in all creation is hidden from God. He sees everything and everyone clearly, without bias, without corruption, and without pretense. No one can hide their motives from God. God is the only wise judge, so let's give up our need to know it all and trust him to do what only he can do.

Can you trust God enough to lay down the right to your judgment of others? Can you do what Jesus called you to and love your neighbor well, as well as love your God with all your heart, soul, mind, and strength? It is not your job to judge your neighbor but to love them. Consider how you can put that into practice and trust God with the rest today.

Wise God, I trust that you see what no one else can. I give up the tendency to judge others and instead open myself up more to your love, and to giving it to others. May I operate in grace and mercy, not in judgment and self-protection.

SEASONS WILL TURN

Rejoice, you people of Jerusalem!
Rejoice in the LORD your God!
For the rain he sends demonstrates his faithfulness.
Once more the autumn rains will come,
as well as the rains of spring.

JOEL 2:23 NLT

If you find yourself longing for winter's end, know that it is coming. The sun rises each morning, bringing with it fresh mercy. The seasons will change, the rains of spring once more bringing signs and songs of hope.

Whatever feels like drudgery, can you bring it into the light of this truth? This too shall pass, and you will find yourself in the long days of bright light and warm air. God is faithful to come through for you, just as you can count on day turning to night and winter giving way to spring. Rest in the hope that you will get through this. Lighter days will soon come upon you.

Faithful One, thank you for the promise of your loyal love meeting me with each new sunrise and every turning of the seasons. I trust you, and I look to you for help and hope.

NEVER ALONE

"I am with you always,
to the end of the age."
MATTHEW 28:20 NASB

The same promise that Christ gave to his disciples before he ascended to the Father's side is the promise we have to hold onto today. We are never without the presence of God through his Spirit. When we yield our lives to Christ, he makes his home in our hearts.

We cannot escape the goodness of God. David knew this truth well when he said, "If I ascend to heaven, You are there; If I make my bed in Sheol, behold You are there" (Psalm 139:8). He is everywhere we are, wherever we go. His mercy is ever-present, and his wisdom is at hand. He is trustworthy and faithful, and we can depend on him every moment of every day. We couldn't evade him if we tried.

Ever-Present one, your presence brings peace, clarity, hope, and joy. I have found my sense of safety and belonging in you. I look to you today, and I hope in your present help. Speak to me as I open up to you and reveal yourself in practical and tangible ways in my life even today, Lord.

OPEN UNDERSTANDING

Then he opened their minds
to understand the Scriptures.
LUKE 24:45 ESV

God gives us clarity for our confusion. He offers solutions for our problems. He opens our minds to understand his truth and his ways. We don't have to try harder to get it; when we look to him as our teacher and leader, he shows us the way.

When you find yourself stumped today, look to the Lord. Ask the Spirit to open your understanding and to give you strategic plans for your problems. He is so faithful to guide us. He is rich in wisdom and is never at a loss for what to do. Wait on him and study his Word. He will reveal his truth as you do.

Wise God, I believe that all problems find a solution in you. I come to you for wisdom, strategy, and help. Open my understanding and reveal your ways in practical steps as I spend time in your Word. I know that your gospel is simple, and I don't want to overcomplicate it. Thank you for your fellowship and for your leadership in my life.

DIVINE EXCHANGE

I will give them a crown to replace their ashes,
and the oil of gladness to replace their sorrow,
and clothes of praise to replace their spirit of sadness.
ISAIAH 61:3 NCV

Though we cannot escape loss in this life, we can trust the one who offers us hope in the midst of it. Trusting God does not mean life becomes pain-free or easy. However, it does mean that we lean on the one who never grows weary in love and who never runs out of what we need.

God is abundant in mercy and generous in redemptive power. He promises crowns for our ashes, joy for our mourning, and garments of praise for our sadness. What an overwhelmingly good God he is. When we are sad, broken-down, and helpless, he offers us the abundant beauty of his presence, his strength, and his peace.

Good God, thank you for the promise of restoration and redemption I find in you. You don't leave me to waste away in the ashes of despair. You lift me up, bind up my wounds, and heal me. Thank you.

DEEP SECRETS

"He reveals deep and secret things;
he knows what is in the darkness,
and light dwells with him."

DANIEL 2:22 NKJV

When we give our lives to knowing God, to walking in his ways and living out his love, he offers us more of himself. Fellowship with God is not something we have to wish for; it is ours through Christ. It is ours in the Spirit. We are met with abundant love every time we turn to him.

Do you want to know what God sees? There is no other way than to get to know him: his character, his presence, and the fruit of his life in ours. He shares his perspective as we surrender to his wisdom. Do you want to know his heart? Become his friend. Friends of God know him like David, Moses, and Abraham. Mary, Paul, and Peter. There have been so many and there will be many more. Will you be one?

Christ, I want to know the deep and secret things of your heart. I want to know you more than anything else. I give myself to know you: to be your faithful friend and your loyal lover. You are so, so worthy of my attention, my time, and my trust.

FEBRUARY

Guard your heart above all else,
for it is the source of life.

PROVERBS 4:23 CSB

COMPLETELY NEW

If anyone is in Christ, he is a new creation:
the old has passed away, and see, the new has come!
2 CORINTHIANS 5:17 CSB

The mistakes of our past have no hold over us if we are in Christ. He has made us completely new in his mercy. He does not hold our sins against us, nor are we defined by what others say about us. We are liberated in love, emerging fresh and new.

Have you ever longed for a fresh start? True fresh starts are hard to come by in this world, but in Christ you have it. His mercy is like a reset; though you can't escape the natural consequences of your choices, he empowers you by his Spirit to move in reconciliation. He completely transforms your heart, your mind, and your life as you yield to his leadership. He is so good, and he is worth surrendering to.

Jesus Christ, thank you for making me a new creation. What I once felt hemmed in by, I am free to move on from. Thank you for breaking the cycles of sin, shame, and fear, and for setting me upon the solid rock of your love. I live for you.

ALWAYS FAITHFUL

The Lord Yahweh is always faithful to place you on a firm
foundation and guard you from the Evil One.

2 THESSALONIANS 3:3 TPT

When you trust in the Lord as your Savior, your strength,
and your guide, you can rest assured that he will always place
you on a firm foundation in times of trouble. Even when the
winds of trouble blow, you can rest in the safety of his love.
He will guard you from the enemy, and he will keep you
steadfast and safe, immovable from his rock of mercy.

Instead of letting anxiety rise as the winds of chaos start
blowing, look to the Lord Yahweh who is ever so near.
Remember that he places your feet on a firm foundation. He
hides you in the cleft of his presence. You will not fear what
comes, for "You can run under his covering of majesty and
hide. His arms of faithfulness are a shield keeping you from
harm" (Psalm 91:4). Rest in him, no matter what happens
today.

Faithful Lord, thank you for offering yourself as my hiding
place. I run into your presence, finding the peace my soul
needs. Place me on a firm foundation and guard me from
the threats that surround. I trust you.

NOURISHED

"Remain in me, as I also remain in you.
No branch can bear fruit by itself;
it must remain in the vine.
Neither can you bear fruit
unless you remain in me."

JOHN 15:4 NIV

Jesus is our life-union with the Father. As we abide in him, he nourishes our lives from the inside out. We cannot bear the fruit of his kingdom apart from him. He is the very source of life, and what he offers is good, pure, life-giving, and refreshing to our souls. His peace pervades our systems as we connect to him.

Instead of trying to push through in your own strength today, lean on the presence of God. Give him time and space to fill you up with his love. Open your heart to him, connect to his presence, and let his grace strengthen your heart, your resolve, and your offering of work. When you are nourished by the connection of Christ, you can't help but bear his fruit.

Christ, thank you for the power of your grace and mercy in my life. I yield to your presence today, and as I do, fill me with the peace, joy, hope, and love of your life in mine. Thank you.

SMALL BEGINNINGS

"Do not despise these small beginnings,
for the LORD rejoices to see the work begin."
ZECHARIAH 4:10 NLT

Small beginnings are nothing to be ashamed of. In fact, most beginnings start out with just a seed: a small, vulnerable idea or dream that needs to be nurtured and shaped into its full form. You don't have to know the full form or every step along the way in order to start or to take the first step.

Instead of being overwhelmed at all the unknowns, embrace the mystery of the future while establishing a clear directive for where you can start today. As you give time and energy to starting the work, as well as continuing to develop it, it will take form as you go. You don't have to know more than what is required right now to take that first beginning step. The wisdom of God is simple, though we often overcomplicate it. Throw off the excuses, the what-ifs, and the complications of things you haven't approached yet and do the small, manageable thing today. The Lord rejoices to see the work begin.

Lord, thank you that I don't need to see the end from the beginning and every step along the way. You do, though, and I trust you to guide me with your wisdom, perspective, and truth. You are a reliable leader.

GOOD THOUGHTS

Whatever is true, whatever is honorable,
whatever is just, whatever is pure, whatever is lovely,
whatever is commendable, if there is any excellence,
if there is anything worthy of praise,
think about these things.

PHILIPPIANS 4:8 ESV

The quality of our thoughts affects our wellbeing. When we are overrun by fear, anxiety, temptation, jealousy, etc., they weigh like burdens on our shoulders. It is hard to walk in the freedom of faith when we are constantly being fed fearful commentaries.

Not every thought we think is what we actually believe. We get to choose which thoughts we align with, and we also get to take control over what we feed our minds and hearts through what we watch, listen to, and entertain in our minds. Consider the criteria laid out in today's verse and use it with intention to align your thoughts with the kingdom of Christ. It is possible to direct your thoughts in line with what God offers, who he is, and what he wants for you. Do the work today, and consider how it affects your relationships, your mood, and your work.

Pure One, help me to take my thoughts captive and focus on the things of your kingdom. Align my thoughts, my heart, and my life in your loving nature. Thank you.

ALONE TIME

"Come away by yourselves to a secluded place and rest a while." (For there were many people coming and going, and they did not even have time to eat.)

MARK 6:31 NASB

Jesus did not spend all his time with others. He knew the power of rest on his energy, perspective, and ability to minister to others. You have not been called to a non-stop hustle and grind. That is not the culture of God's kingdom.

Instead of burning yourself out and bending to the wishes of others at all times of day, take the advice of Jesus and come away by yourself to a secluded place and rest a while. Whether in the beginning, middle or end of your day, prioritize a time of dedicated rest where you can be alone and center yourself in the ability to choose what is best for you. Allow Christ to minister to you as you quiet the noise of others' demands and rest in his peace. He will refresh you in his presence as you do.

Jesus, thank you for the example of prioritizing rest and alone time in your ministry. I don't want to give so much of myself that I lose connection with who I am, who you are, and who you've called me to be. I love you.

PATTERNS OF LIFE

"From the beginning I told you what would happen in the end.
A long time ago I told you things that have not yet happened.
When I plan something, it happens.
What I want to do, I will do."

ISAIAH 46:10 NCV

It can be frustrating to weather hard times when we saw our lives going differently. Transition and change are as much a part of life as development and aging. We can't avoid them. When we feel like things have completely gone off-track in our lives, God is never at a loss, and his promises do not void.

What God said he will do, he does. It may not happen on our timeline or in the ways we expect, but he is faithful nevertheless. Think through your life. Can you remember a hope you had that you now are living in the reality of? How is the reality different than your expectations? Just because your life hasn't unfolded in the way you thought it would, it doesn't mean it is any less valuable or beautiful. Hold onto hope. God will bring all the pieces of your life together and he will fulfill his promises to you.

Faithful Father, I'm so grateful you aren't surprised by the things that throw me off. Your perspective is perfect, and your loyalty is undeterred. I trust you.

WHAT YOU NEED

If any of you lacks wisdom, he should ask God,
who gives to all generously and ungrudgingly,
and it will be given to him.
JAMES 1:5 CSB

It is not selfish to ask for what you need. You don't need to try harder or do everything yourself. You were not made to be self-sufficient. You were created to thrive in family and community. God is your Father, and he is not distant. Do you need wisdom? Ask him for it and he will gladly share his perspective with you.

Practice asking for help when you find you are at a loss. Reach out to those around you who are skilled and able to help you. You are not a burden when you share a need with others. You are not meant to figure things out on your own. You can grow and thrive in connecting to others and by learning from them. Make it a point to ask for something you need help with today.

Wise God, thank you for your wealth of wisdom. Just as I've learned to come to you with an open heart, help me to be open in reaching out to others for help when I need it.

PRODUCTIVE TRUST

Blessed is the man who trusts in the LORD,
and whose hope is the LORD.
For he shall be like a tree planted by the waters,
which spreads out its roots by the river,
and will not fear when heat comes;
but its leaf will be green,
and will not be anxious in the year of drought,
nor will cease from yielding fruit.

JEREMIAH 17:7-8 NKJV

Trusting in the Lord does not mean that we ignore the realities of our lives or the world at large. It doesn't mean that we check out of our responsibilities to one another, either. It is a posture of faith. Trust is a deeply rooted conviction that God is faithful and good, and he will continue to be reliable in love.

True trust yields fruitfulness in our lives. It is a source of abundant life, refreshing peace, and obstinate hope. As we remain connected to the source of mercy-kindness and goodness, we persist in producing the fruits of the Spirit, no matter what challenges we face. Thank God that he remains the same and his love never lets up from our lives.

Trustworthy One, I choose to put the anchor of my trust in your unchanging character. Move in me, Spirit of God, and produce your fruit in my surrendered life.

THE LIVING EXPRESSION

The Living Expression became a man and lived among us!
And we gazed upon his glory, the glory of the One and Only
who came from the Father overflowing with tender mercy
and truth!

JOHN 1:14 TPT

If we wonder what God truly looks like—his character and
personality—we have no further to look than the life of
Jesus Christ. Through the lens of history, we do not have a
full picture, but we certainly have the flesh and bones: the
glimpse of God in human form.

As we look at the life of Jesus, reading the gospels and
fellowshipping with his Spirit, we are able to see the
breakdown of what once was thought about God and
what Jesus revealed about him. Jesus revealed that God
is merciful: much more merciful than what was once
understood. He is not concerned with how a person presents
themselves but with the intentions of their heart. Let's gaze
upon the glory of Christ even now, for as we do, we will be
transformed by his living truth and tender mercy.

Lord Jesus, thank you for breaking down the walls of
misunderstanding of who God is in the traditions of man.
You are better than they hoped, and you remain better than
I have yet experienced. Thank you.

CHOOSE YOUR MEASURE

"Give, and it will be given to you.
A good measure, pressed down, shaken together
and running over, will be poured into your lap.
For with the measure you use, it will be measured to you."

LUKE 6:38 NIV

One of the main principles of the kingdom of God revealed through Jesus is generosity. Give, and it will be given to you. The Passion Translation says it this way: "Give generously and generous gifts will be given back to you." You will receive in the same measure that you give. If you give a little, you can expect to receive a little in return.

How do you approach the use of your finances? Is your mentality to scrimp and save or to hoard what you have away? Perhaps you live within your means, but you don't often offer to help others. It may be beneficial to put yourself in the shoes of someone in need. God so generously offers grace and mercy from the abundance of his being. How can you partner with his generosity in practical ways today?

Generous One, I know I have room to stretch my generosity, and I want to. Help me to be practical in showing love to others, without needing anything from them in return. I trust that you see my sacrifice and gifts and you will be the one to offer the greatest return.

OVERFLOW OF GOODNESS

"A good person produces good things from the treasury of a good heart, and an evil person produces evil things from the treasury of an evil heart. What you say flows from what is in your heart."

LUKE 6:45 NLT

Our lives reflect what is going on in our hearts. If we have goodness, mercy, and peace in our hearts, it will overflow into what we produce with our hands. If we want to live good lives as good people, then the work starts within us.

As we yield our hearts to the Lord, following his lead and adopting his ways, he transforms us in his palpable love. Love always makes a difference. It is the most powerful force in the universe. The mercy of God meets us where we are today. It reaches beyond the outer circumstances of our lives into the deepest reaches of our hearts. There, he ministers to us with kindness and encourages us to stand upon his faithful truth. From the mouth the heart speaks, so let's yield our hearts to him.

Good Father, I want my life to reflect your nature and values. I know that you are loving, patient, kind, and just. You are gracious. Heal my heart and let it reflect your powerful mercy as I live, speak, and interact with others. I want to overflow with goodness.

FOLLOW HIM

"You shall follow the LORD your God and fear him;
and you shall keep His commandments,
listen to his voice, serve him, and cling to him."

DEUTERONOMY 13:4 NASB

When you focus your attention on following the Lord, it will affect how you see the world. The difference between how God operates and how the systems of this world do is stark. God is gracious and merciful, and man-made systems are often harsh and exclusive.

When you find yourself frustrated by how things in this world work, look to the one who does all things well. He is perfect in nature, and he won't let you down. He doesn't make it harder to find him; he offers his love and wisdom to those who seek it. Christ's death removed every single hindrance that kept God's presence from the people, as evidenced in the veil being torn in two in the holy of holies. There is now nothing that can separate you from his love.

Father, my hope is in you, not in the systems of this world. They will always fail, but your ways never do. I choose to trust you and follow you all the days of my life.

GLORIOUS GRACE

By grace you have been saved through faith,
and that not of yourselves; it is the gift of God.
EPHESIANS 2:8 NKJV

God's grace is outrageous. If it doesn't seem extravagant to us, we have more yet to experience and understand it. God's grace never runs out. We don't earn it—not ever. And it is not a one-time experience. God offers us grace upon grace, as the Scriptures tell us. He is generous in every moment.

Christ's fullness is our source of grace. When we approach our Savior, even with a turning of our attention to him, he meets us with grace. His mercy is plentiful. Do you feel as if you've taken advantage of the Lord's kindness? Even if you could, he offers you fresh mercy today. He is not weak in love, but strong in it. He does not need your surrender, but he loves to shower you with his goodness as you submit to him. All that Christ requires of you is for your benefit. It is for your good. Be renewed in his glorious grace as you come to him with an open heart.

Gracious God, I have tasted of your goodness, but I know there is so much more to learn about you. Take me as I am today and renew my life, my passion, and my heart in your limitless love. Thank you.

PERFECT ONE

"This God, his way is perfect;
the word of the LORD proves true;
he is a shield for all those who take refuge in him."

2 SAMUEL 22:31 ESV

In our humanity, we know what weakness is. We experience our limits as we come to the end of ourselves over and over again. How resilient is the human spirit, but oh how perfect the Spirit of God is! He never errs or leads us astray. He is always right, always good, and always true.

This can be a tremendous comfort to us when we are disappointed by those in our lives. Though our parents did not always do things perfectly, God is the perfect parent. Though our friends may hurt us, Christ is the perfect friend. Though our governments may fail us in a myriad of ways, God is a perfect and righteous King. Whenever we feel the sting of our limitations in relationship, let's find solace in the Perfect One who never changes.

Righteous King, there isn't a role that you don't fit perfectly. You are the most faithful friend, sticking closer than blood. You are the perfect parent, even in the ways you train and discipline us in kindness. You are better than anyone I've ever known, and I rest in you.

COMPELLING CURIOSITY

"Everyone who asks will receive.
The one who searches will find.
And everyone who knocks will have the door opened."
LUKE 11:10 NCV

Prayer is how we connect to God. Spirit to Spirit we fellowship with the presence of God as we pour our hearts out to him. Why then wouldn't we ask for what is on our heart? Why would we not search for the goodness of God in the world around us? Curiosity—about the world, about God, about anything—is welcomed in the presence of God. He does not ask us to edit ourselves with him. He wants us as we are: wholly imperfect and full of questions.

When was the last time you directed your questions to the Lord? The one who searches will find. As you search out God's wisdom, not only in Scripture, but also in the sciences, in social situations, and in nature, you will find it. You know what God is like; the fruit of his Spirit makes that clear. Can you not use that as a measure in your prayer life and in the way you live?

Lord, I have experienced skepticism of curiosity, but I don't want that to keep me from living open-heartedly in the world. You don't shut down my questions; you welcome them. Thank you.

GENEROUS LIVING

One person gives freely,
yet gains more;
another withholds what is right,
only to become poor.

PROVERBS 11:24 CSB

Being stingy with our resources does not equate to wisdom,
nor does it guarantee our peace. When we withhold what
is owed, we are the ones who suffer. When we refuse to
help those in need when we are able, we miss out on the
opportunity to partner with God's heart.

Think of the most generous person you know. What about
their lifestyle do you respect? Which things could you
implement in your own life, even if on a smaller scale?
Nobody can make you become generous. It is something
that you must choose. If you desire to expand your heart and
life in this way, ask the Spirit to help you. Just know, when it
comes down to it, only you can choose to do it. Generosity
does not work as a theory, only as an active practice.

Great God, I want to be more generous than I currently am
because you are and because I know the wonderful gift it
is to partner with you. Help me to take practical steps in
generosity today.

SOWING INTO FRIENDSHIP

Sweet friendships refresh the soul
and awaken our hearts with joy,
for good friends are like the anointing oil
that yields the fragrant incense of God's presence.
PROVERBS 27:9 TPT

Relationships make our lives rich. They are the spaces in which we get to incorporate our deepest selves: being seen, known, and accepted as we are. They are also the places where we grow, for none of us is the same and we get to learn from one another.

Who are the people you are grateful for in this life? Proverbs says that sweet friendships refresh the soul and awaken our hearts with joy. When you consider who leaves you feeling refreshed and filled with joy, who are those friends? The quantity of friendships doesn't matter, but the quality of those relationships does. Sow into your friendships and celebrate the beauty that comes from such sweet fellowship.

Lord, you know all about friendship. You created me to both know others and be known. Thank you for the people who bring refreshing and peace to my life. I'm so grateful for each of them. As I consider the best friends I have, I cannot neglect your friendship. Oh, how I long to know you more.

AN OPEN BOOK

All my longings lie open before you, LORD;
my sighing is not hidden from you.
PSALM 38:9 NIV

One of the most powerful truths of knowing the Lord is that he sees us just as we are, without pretense or misgiving. We don't have to pretend to be happier than we are at any given moment. And still, God offers us rest and relief in the comforting presence of his Spirit.

Authenticity doesn't mean that we drown in despair when things are hard. It doesn't mean that we ignore others' sorrow when our lives are bursting with joy. Authenticity is just showing up as we are, and that does not take away from anyone else's experience of life. This might be something that we first begin to practice in our relationship with the Lord. When we are tempted to ignore our hearts, we can instead choose to lay them open bare before the Lord. We can offer him the questions and longings, for he sees them regardless. What a relief to know that the Lord hears the cries of our hearts, and he answers them.

Lord, I trust that you see my heart as it is, and you meet me where I am. I don't want to hide myself from you, not any part of me. Read my longings and answer the cries of my heart.

FILLED UP

I pray that God, the source of all hope, will fill you completely with joy and peace because you trust in him. Then you will overflow with confident hope through the power of the Holy Spirit.

ROMANS 15:13 NLT

As we trust in the Lord, he fills us completely with his joy and peace. What a promise! He is the source of all hope, not only ours but the entire world's. As God fills us up with his plentiful peace and uplifting joy, we also overflow with confident hope in every area of our lives. It is a beautiful reaction to God's work in us.

Ask the Spirit to deepen your trust and to exude through your life his powerful peace. It is not something that can be manufactured; it is the work of the Spirit in your life. It is mysterious and wonderful. Whatever areas you feel depleted, the Lord has abundant grace, love, and joy to offer you. Only open and up and receive. There is a river of goodness flowing from the Father's heart into your life today.

Glorious God, you are the source of all that I need. You see where I am running dry. Fill me up to overflow with your peace, joy, and love today.

COURAGEOUS HOPE

Be strong, and let your heart take courage,
all you who wait for the LORD!
PSALM 31:24 ESV

Why should our hearts take courage in God today? In verse 23 of Psalm 31, directly before today's verse, it says, "Love the Lord… [he] preserves the faithful but abundantly repays the one who acts in pride." If we love the Lord with our hearts, souls, mind, and strength, then we love God with our lives. If we love him with our lives, we remain faithful to his ways. If we remain faithful to his ways, we can be confident and courageous, knowing that the Lord will break through for us.

God is faithful; that is the basis of our trust. He does all that he says he will do. He remains consistent in loyal love and powerful mercy. He cannot change, and he will not change his mind. What he promises, he will accomplish. What a reason to be strong of heart and courageously confident today.

Faithful Father, I yield my understanding to you. I know that you are greater than I can imagine, but I want to know you in Spirit and in truth. I offer you my heart and life. I'm placing all my bets on you.

REDEEMED AND EMBRACED

"I have redeemed you;
I have called you by name;
you are Mine!"

ISAIAH 43:1 NASB

When we know that we belong to the King of kings and Lord of lords, it reflects in our mindsets, our relationships, and our lifestyles. Meditate on today's verse. Read it as if God is speaking to you here and now, for he is.

Christ is your Redeemer. He has called you his own. The Father has welcomed you as his child. He has given you his name: the seal of his mercy is on your life. He has given you a new name and a new identity in his kingdom. He offers you the refuge of his kingdom, and he will never turn you away from his table. Come to him, fellowship with him. Be embraced by his love. Feast on his goodness. He has redeemed you, calling you by name. You are his!

Redeemer, thank you for embracing me as your own. Thank you for covering my life with the power of your restorative love. Thank you for who you are to me, and who I am to you. I am filled with your pervasive peace. You are my home, and I am who you say I am—your child. Father, I delight in you.

COME TO YOUR FATHER

"He arose and came to his father.
But when he was still a great way off,
his father saw him and had compassion,
and ran and fell on his neck and kissed him."

LUKE 15:20 NKJV

In the parable of the prodigal son, Jesus illustrated how loving the Father is. No matter how much of your inheritance you feel you have squandered, God is waiting to run to meet you as you turn to him. He has royal robes to wrap around you. He will not ignore you or disown you. He waits patiently for you to approach him. And as you come, he runs to meet you while you are still on your way.

There isn't any mistake, fear, or shame that need keep you from turning to your good Father. He has not grown tired of loving you. In fact, he longs to embrace you in his mercy. Throw off what holds you back and turn to him today.

Good Father, your mercy is unmatched, and your love is overwhelmingly good. Thank you for embracing me, redeeming me, and calling me your own. I won't stay away from your presence, for you are indescribably kind to me.

SHARE GOOD NEWS

"Go into all the world
and preach the gospel to all creation."
MARK 16:15 CSB

Good news is worth being shared with as many people
as you can. We get enough of bad news in daily life from
reports around the world, we hear of wars, crimes, and
schemes. How could it change your outlook to focus on
sharing good news with others today?

Consider what you spend your emotional energy on. What
kind of news are you mostly focusing on? What is the fruit of
the sources you listen to on a daily basis? Instead of allowing
fear-based reports to set you on edge and lose your hope,
tune into what breathes encouragement, life, and hope into
your heart. You don't have to disconnect from reality to
maintain hope, but you should be intentional about what
you allow to influence you. Lastly, don't forget how your
perception can affect others.

Merciful King, I know that where there are reports of bad
news, there is also goodness at work. Your miraculous
mercy is always working even through seasons of drought
and winter. May I be a bearer of the truth of your good
news, no matter what is going on in the world.

WONDERFUL WISDOM

The wisdom that comes from God is first of all pure, then peaceful, gentle, and easy to please. This wisdom is always ready to help those who are troubled and to do good for others. It is always fair and honest.

JAMES 3:17 NCV

The wisdom of God is full of the fruit of God's presence. It is pure, peaceful, gentle, and easy to please. It is ready to help those who are in trouble and to always do good for others. It is honest at all times. It is fair, not giving shortcuts to some and barriers to others. If the wisdom you receive or give is anything less than this, it does not come from God.

Instead of focusing our attention on the things that divide, corrode, and disrupt us, let's look to God for his solutions. He always is willing to share his pure wisdom with those who seek him. He is easy to please, not giving us hoops to jump through. He will not lie to us, nor will he instruct us to treat others in any way but with love. His ways are better than our ways, and his thoughts are higher than our thoughts.

God, I want to be consumed with your wisdom, not my own opinions or the opinions of others. I want to walk in the freedom of your love that leads with kindness, honesty, peace, and joy.

FEED YOUR MIND

Perfect, absolute peace surrounds those
whose imaginations are consumed with you;
they confidently trust in you.
ISAIAH 26:3 TPT

When our imaginations are consumed with the truth of who
God is, we can rest in the perfect peace of his loyal love. God
is faithful, he is just, and he is merciful. We won't ever wake
up to him changing his mind. He is constant, true, and he is
trustworthy.

Whether through reading Scripture, praying, or listening
to worship music, direct your imagination toward the Lord
in all of his greatness and goodness today. As you feed your
mind with the beautiful nature of Christ, your heart will
grow in hope as the roots of your faith grow deeper into the
soil of his love. He never fails, and he won't stop now.

Lord, I direct my attention to you over and over again.
Each time I do, expand my understanding of you, even as
my imagination stretches to contain more of who you are.
I will feast on the power of your unchanging character and
meditate on your mercy-kindness.

APPLICATION MATTERS

"Blessed rather are those who hear the word of God
and obey it."
LUKE 11:28 NIV

It is not enough to believe something with your intellect. In order to truly adopt it, you must act on it. We are bombarded with information day and night. If we didn't want to, we would never need to take a break from ingesting others' opinions, news, or entertainment. But we weren't built for this type of overload. We need down time and space to implement what we value.

It takes time to learn and integrate things into our lives. It's not a matter of perfectly performing from the start, but of making habits and putting things into practice. If we truly treasure the wisdom of God, we cannot simply say we do. We need to do what God says. We are so very blessed when we do, as Jesus said.

Gracious Jesus, thank you for your wisdom and your patience. As I put your ways into practice in my life, direct me on the path of your laid-down-love. I choose to follow you because I know that you are the way, the truth, and the life.

GOOD CONNECTIONS

Every time I think of you,
I give thanks to my God.
PHILIPPIANS 1:3 NLT

When we are focused on the things that we lack, we can become disappointed by what we don't have. However, if we take time to account for the good things in life, an attitude of gratitude can lift our spirits and rejuvenate our hope.

Think through the people in your life that have positively impacted you. Who are the ones, who like Paul said, you are thankful for every time you think of them? Reach out to them with a text, a phone call, or a card. Celebrate their influence in your life, for they are gifts of God to you. Find ways to connect with them, and others, in meaningful ways as you go about your day. Good relationships are the richest treasures we experience in this life.

My God, thank you for the wonderful people you have placed in my life to bring encouragement, hope, and comfort. I cannot thank you enough for the power of their impact in my life. May I focus on what I can sow into relationships rather than getting caught up in to-dos today. Thank you.

MARCH

We destroy every proud obstacle
that keeps people from knowing
God. We capture their rebellious
thoughts and teach them to
obey Christ.

2 Corinthians 10:5 NLT

REASONS TO REJOICE

This is the day which the LORD has made;
let us rejoice and be glad in it.

PSALM 118:24 NASB

Perhaps you have heard the old song that is based off of Psalm 118:24. I, for one, cannot help but hear the psalmist's words being sung as I read today's verse. *This is the day, this is the day that the Lord has made.*

How can you rejoice in the day that the Lord has made? Look for the goodness, like a treasure-hunt if need be, and be glad for each bit you find. Today is all you have. You can't reach into yesterday or pull yourself into tomorrow. Find peace, gratitude, and joy in the present moment. It is a gift. It is a new day, a new month, and a new start. Receive the goodness that God offers through his matchless mercy. He is near, and his fingerprints of mercy are not difficult to find.

Faithful One, thank you for today; it is a fresh start and a reason to give thanks. I want to rejoice in the goodness of your presence all day long. Reveal yourself to me as I look for hints of your nearness in all areas of my life.

SHAME INTO PRAISE

"Behold, at that time I will deal
with all your oppressors.
And I will save the lame
and gather the outcast,
and I will change their shame into praise
and renown in all the earth."

ZEPHANIAH 3:19 ESV

The Lord our God is worthy of trust. He remembers every promise he has ever made, and he follows through on each one. He will deal with the oppressors of this world. He saves the lame and gathers the outcast—every single one. He takes our shame and turns it into reasons to praise. He is wonderful.

Whatever hard circumstances you are dealing with, know that God is with you, and he is for you. Life may make a mess of your perfect dreams, but the redemption of God weaves together a beautiful tapestry of his wonders through the details of your life. Trust him and lean on his presence. He will not leave you to waste away, for he is your Savior and Redeemer, and he is faithful.

Redeemer, thank you for the hope of your salvation. I trust you to come through for me in practical and supernatural ways. I choose to follow you because you are worthy, and you are worth it.

RETURN

Let the wicked one abandon his way
and the sinful one his thoughts;
let him return to the LORD,
so he may have compassion on him,
and to our God, for he will freely forgive.

ISAIAH 55:7 CSB

It is always time to turn (and return) to the Lord. It is always the right moment to come to him. No matter how short or long it's been, the Lord welcomes you with an overflowing heart of mercy. He longs to lift the burdens from your shoulders and forgive what you have trouble letting go of.

He is a tremendously good Father. He is full of kindness and compassion. He has strategies to help you overcome the hurdles in your life. He has comfort for your pain, strength for your weakness, and hope for your despair. Don't stay away from him when you can be engulfed fully in his loving embrace today.

Merciful Father, I cannot begin to thank you for your kindness toward me. I love you, and I trust you. As I come to you, lift the heavy burdens I offer and wash me anew in the living waters of your presence.

A BETTER STANDARD

"The LORD does not see as man sees;
for man looks at the outward appearance,
but the LORD looks at the heart."

1 SAMUEL 16:7 NKJV

Though we are given to judge others quickly and superficially, God does neither. The Lord sees through our outer appearance into the intentions of our heart. He knows what we are made of. The heart is what moves a person to action. It is where we dream and hope, and where some scheme and plot.

Regardless of how well put-together or careless we appear, God does not base his opinion of us on how we look. Our stature, abilities, and talents don't impress or deter him. He lovingly guides the humble of heart, and he teaches those who long to know his truth. We don't have to strive to find our place in the world, for we have already been established in Christ. With our feet on the firm foundation of his mercy, we are free to follow him.

Lord Jesus, your ways, your thoughts, and your judgments are better than those of this world. I don't want to impress others only to find that I've lost myself in the process. Root and ground me in your love that I may flourish as I was always meant to.

CHILDLIKE

"Let the little children come to me.
Don't stop them, because the kingdom of God
belongs to people who are like these children."
LUKE 18:16 NCV

The next time you are around a child, consider what it means to be childlike. Perhaps you already know well: they are open, vulnerable, and curious. They can be inquisitive and hyper-focused. They can be silly and creative. They may be annoying. These are just a few attributes, but they are all true of children at different times.

Just as Jesus welcomed the little children to come to him with the messiness of their authenticity, so Jesus welcomes you in the same way. You don't have to dress yourself up or act differently. You don't have to pretend to understand what you have not yet learned. You don't have to silence your questions. Simply come to him, for he welcomes you with open arms.

Wonderful Jesus, thank you for welcoming me as I am. I want to allow my childlike curiosity and wonder to grow, just as you do. I am yours, and I come running to you today.

DESIGNED WITH DESTINY

We have become his poetry, a re-created people that will
fulfill the destiny he has given each of us, for we are joined
to Jesus, the Anointed One. Even before we were born, God
planned in advance our destiny and the good works we
would do to fulfill it!

EPHESIANS 2:10 TPT

Each of us was created with purpose. It doesn't have to look
like anyone else's life to matter to God and to us. We were
knit together with creativity, unique personalities, and a
hunger to learn and connect with others.

As we join our lives to Jesus, we don't lose this sense of
purpose. In fact, we gain it. He has already planned out the
good works we can do in this life. As we partner with his
nature, he partners with us in sowing seeds of mercy, of
peace, and of redemption. Let's not overlook the simple ways
we can make a difference: to love and allow ourselves to be
loved, to give to those in need, and to have integrity. Though
our lives will look different, the poetry of God's pen writes
through our lived-out surrender.

Creator, thank you for designing me with a purpose. I am
not a mistake, and I don't have to be like anyone else around
me. Thank you for the power of your love that liberates me
to live fully as the person you've created me to be.

GIVER OF GOOD GIFTS

Every good and perfect gift is from above,
coming down from the Father of the heavenly lights,
who does not change like shifting shadows.

JAMES 1:17 NIV

Do you believe that God is good? Really think about it. What are the things you assume about God's character? It is helpful to know what misgivings you may have about him so that you can allow him to change your mind, if necessary. There are some beliefs we have because of the Scriptures, while others are because of tradition, bias, and limited experience. Will you allow yourself to admit that you don't see the whole picture? When you are able to do this, you humble your heart and soften it to be able to change.

Every good and perfect gift is from above. Every miracle of mercy in your life, every good friend, every relief or comfort that has brought you closer to love and peace reflects a kind and good Father. Allow yourself to count your blessings today, if for no other reason than to see that there are good gifts already in your life.

Good Father, I humble my heart before you knowing I have so much to learn still. Teach me your ways. I want to know who you truly are—in Spirit and in truth. Open my eyes to the enormity of your goodness in my life already. Thank you.

CONSIDER THIS

"Do to others as you would
like them to do to you."
LUKE 6:31 NLT

Jesus gave us the "golden rule" when he told us to do to
others as we would like them to do to us. This is what we
should measure our actions by. When we are tempted to
be hasty and retaliate against those who have hurt us, we
can instead remember what Christ said. If we wouldn't like
others to treat us that way, we probably shouldn't, either.

We can never do this perfectly, but the point is that we
try. Even when we fail, we can repair and restore through
humility and forgiveness. We cannot demand others forgive
us. This is all an inner work. We cannot control the choices
of others; we can only choose how we will move. Let's take
responsibility of our actions and align them with the law of
love that Christ so powerfully taught.

Jesus, help me to walk in the light of your love, giving the
benefit of the doubt, offering grace and mercy. I choose to
follow you and adopt your ways, because they are right,
true, and always for the good of all.

ENLIGHTENED IN HOPE

I pray that the eyes of your heart may be enlightened,
so that you will know what is the hope of his calling,
what are the riches of the glory of his inheritance in the saints.
EPHESIANS 1:18 NASB

Another way to talk about the eyes of your heart is to speak
of your imagination. Paul prayed that the Ephesians would
be able to enlarge their imaginations in the Spirit of God.
Then they would know the great hope of their calling, and
the riches of Christ's glorious inheritance in the saints.

As the eyes of your heart open in revelatory understanding—
imagining even beyond what you have yet seen, known,
or experienced—your hope will expand. You will catch
glimpses of the glorious goodness that awaits you in the
fullness of Christ's kingdom. It will all be worth it: every
sacrifice and surrender. Every hope and every longing. He is
so much better than any of us could imagine.

Great One, I want the eyes of my heart to open in
understanding, and to stretch in awe and wonder. You are
glorious, and I know one day I will see you fully. I wait and
long for that day to come. In the meantime, show me more
of who you are.

POWER OF FAITH

"Truly, I say to you, if you have faith like a grain of mustard seed, you will say to this mountain, 'Move from here to there,' and it will move, and nothing will be impossible for you."

MATTHEW 17:20 ESV

You don't need a large amount of faith to make a difference. You don't need to know the details of the future in order to move ahead one step. Jesus said that even the smallest seed of faith could move a mountain from its place. Let's not underestimate the power of faith, no matter how little it is.

What is faith? Hebrews 11:1 defines it as "the assurance of things hoped for, the conviction of things not seen." In fact, the entirety of Hebrews 11 is an account of what faith looked like in the lives of those who have gone before: the heroes, so to speak, of our faith. When Abraham left his home for an unknown inheritance, he didn't know where he would end up. He did, however, trust the one who called him. As we grow deeper in our relationship with God, we are more apt to trust him and to deepen our faith as we follow his ways and his leading.

Faithful One, I'm so glad you don't require more of me than I am able to give. I start here, in this place with you. Speak to me, and I will listen.

LEARNING FROM HISTORY

Whatever was written in the past was written for our instruction, so that we may have hope through endurance and through the encouragement from the Scriptures.

ROMANS 15:4 CSB

When we approach life as if we have to figure everything out on our own, in our own timing, we miss out on the wisdom of those who have gone before us. Generational community is so important. Those who have already lived their own struggles can offer us wisdom and guidance through our own. We don't have to begin from scratch.

It is important that we take lessons from history, and not just the stories we've been told. History holds within it the power of perspective. May we learn from the mistakes of others, just as we learn from their triumphs. There is so much encouragement within Scripture, and there is always hope in the love of Christ working through the ages. As we approach history with an open heart, we will find the mercy of God there to lead us in his wisdom.

Almighty God, I don't want to struggle to understand what you so willingly teach. Open my heart and understanding as I partner with your heart and purposes.

EVERY SINGLE MORNING

I have hope when I think of this:
the LORD's love never ends;
his mercies never stop.
They are new every morning.

LAMENTATIONS 3:21-23 NCV

Today is a brand new day. Allow that to sink in. Let the regrets of yesterday fade away as you focus your attention on the fresh mercy of God with you now. He is not lacking in all that you need. Fill up on his grace, his peace, his joy, whatever you need more of. He is overflowing with generous kindness, and he does not wane in strength.

He sees as clearly today as he did yesterday. Recall the last time you felt a sense of deep relief. That is what you can have in the powerful presence of God right here and now. As you offer him your worries and cares, he lifts the weight of your burdens. He gives you clarity for confusion and strength for weakness. He never offers a stale gift or promise. It is always what is needed: new and fresh to meet you as you are in this moment.

Merciful One, thank you for always knowing exactly what I need at any given moment. I want to know your right-now love and the power of your thoughts over me. Thank you.

POSTURE OF TRUST

Preserve me, O God,
for in you I put my trust.
PSALM 16:1 NKJV

God is a safe place in every trouble. As we run to him, even when it feels like life-or-death, he becomes our refuge of peace. No matter what happens, no one can take away his prevalent peace. No one can remove us from his love.

What do you need God's preservation for? Are there struggles or temptations that you feel vulnerable toward? You can trust God's Spirit to help you. You can lean on the help of good friends to keep you stable. And even when you fall, the grace of God is your landing pad. Don't let shame, fear, or regret keep you from coming to him. He is patient with you, and he is able to empower you to stand. Trust him.

God, I put my trust in you. When I am afraid, weak, and just a big old mess, I run to you. Surround me with your presence of peace and settle my heart in the clarity of your love. You are my God, and I run to you.

EVEN IN HEARTBREAK

He heals the wounds of every shattered heart.
PSALM 147:3 TPT

None of us can escape the pain of heartbreak in this life. We lose those we love in a myriad of ways. We cannot escape death, and we certainly cannot outrun grief. Grief shatters our hearts, but God is the healer of every broken heart. He does not patch us back together haphazardly, either.

Grief can be a breaking open. In that expansive, if devastating, time we have more space to hold the love of God. It reaches into every crack and crevice, sowing new life as our healer restores our hearts and hope in him. He is faithful to do it. No matter how devastated we are, we are not broken beyond repair. We are not too far gone to know peace, hope, and joy again. Though we cannot escape the pain of grief, we can know the power of God's mercy in it.

Healer, you are the one who knit me together in the first place, and you can knit my shattered heart together again. I can never go back to the way it was, but you bring me further into the realms of your kindness—places I never knew existed. Thank you.

COVENANT OF LOVE

"Know therefore that the LORD your God is God;
he is the faithful God, keeping his covenant of love
to a thousand generations of those who love him
and keep his commandments."

DEUTERONOMY 7:9 NIV

God keeps his covenant of love. In our day and age, promises
are made and broken all the time. But God never breaks
a promise. His nature doesn't allow for it. He is faithful,
merciful, and just. He will never forget what he has said, nor
will he change his mind.

The power of God's covenant reaches outside our lives to all
who look to him. Everyone who follows him is covered by his
mercy. We cannot venture to control what this looks like for
anyone. We must let the love of God be as vast and powerful
as he is. As we partner with him, loving the way that Christ
instructed us to, we only have our own choices to account for.
The effects of our choices, however, are far-reaching.

Powerful One, your love is the most potent force on the
planet. It creates space where fear restricts. It sows new life
where condemnation kills. Thank you that your covenant of
love is still going strong.

SEEDS OF ETERNITY

God has made everything beautiful for its own time.
He has planted eternity in the human heart,
but even so, people cannot see the whole scope
of God's work from beginning to end.

ECCLESIASTES 3:11 NLT

Our hearts long for significance. When the young die too soon, we grieve for what could and should have been. Even when the old are ready to let go from this life, there is a longing for more. These are seeds of eternity planted within our hearts.

We cannot know the scope of God's work in the world, but we can certainly find ourselves within his mercy. There is always hope. As long as we have breath there are sunsets to chase and loved ones to embrace. Instead of focusing on what we don't have, let's see the beauty in what is ours now and look with hope to the promise of God's eternal kingdom. We won't miss out on what he has for us, for in fullness we will know him. If not now, then.

God, I believe that you are good, you are powerful, and you are always working in mighty mercy. When I can't make sense of violence, wars, or diagnoses, I still trust in you. You are faithful, and I will dwell with you in the land of your eternal kingdom.

NOT MINE

"LORD our God, all this abundance that we have provided to build You a house for Your holy name, it is from Your hand, and all is Yours."

1 CHRONICLES 29:16 NASB

When we approach life with an open heart of reciprocity, we recognize the gifts we are given and how we can offer them back in kind. We can partner with those who have come before, with the bounty of the land, and with the heart of God. As we do, we use the gifts we have, including talents, resources, and privileges, to give back to others.

If everything finds its source in God, then everything belongs to him. Why would we hoard what was never ours to begin with? As we open our hearts and hands, we allow ourselves to honor both God and the gift, instead of simply being consumers. In fact, it is important that we consider the source of all that we have so that we don't strip our world of all its wonders or use it for our own entertainment. If it all belongs to God, then we should respect it all, too.

Creator, I don't want to live as a mindless consumer of things. I want to partner with your heart and purposes by honoring the gifts you have given and the privilege of the role I can play in offering it back to you in ways that reflect your love.

DELIGHT IN LOVE

This is the love of God, that we keep his commandments.
And his commandments are not burdensome.

1 JOHN 5:3 ESV

The law of God's love does not weigh us down as a burden.
It actually becomes a delight as we live it out. It won't always
feel easy, but God's grace empowers us to choose his ways,
for they are loving and beneficial to all.

As you approach your workload today, what if you looked
for ways to infuse it with love? How could you delight in
what is yours to do instead of dread it? The love of God isn't
reserved for spiritual tasks. It reaches us in every part of our
lives, including the very practical aspects. When you look for
ways to lean into the grace of God with hope, curiosity, and
joy, you partner with his love in living it out.

Gracious God, I want to know the delight of following you
and partnering with you. What has felt like a duty filled with
obligation, lighten the load and show me how to approach it
light-heartedly and with love as my motivation. Thank you.

SHINE ON

You are a chosen people, royal priests, a holy nation, a people
for God's own possession. You were chosen to tell about the
wonderful acts of God, who called you out of darkness into
his wonderful light.

1 PETER 2:9 NCV

Every person who comes to Christ is showered with his love.
The light of his glorious presence shines on all in the same
measure. He does not favor one of his children more than
any other. He loves perfectly, thoroughly, and with such great
measure that we cannot even fathom its enormity.

Think about it this way. If we are stars in the universe, he is our
sun. All that we are and do reflects from the source of his fiery
glory. We can shine confidently for we are reflections of his
light. As we partner with God, we direct the glory back to him;
we can't help but do so. We shine because he shines on us.

Glorious One, thank you for the light of your love that
shines brightly in my life. I confidently shine as you created
me and partner with your heart and ways. You are glorious.

RENEWED IN WAITING

Those who trust in the LORD
will renew their strength;
they will soar on wings like eagles;
they will run and not become weary,
they will walk and not faint.

ISAIAH 40:31 CSB

When waiting seasons come, we cannot speed up the process and time it takes to move ahead. That does not mean that waiting is wasted. We rest and restore in God's presence. He renews our strength as we wait on him.

However short or long the waiting is, it is worth it to press in to the Lord's presence. Consider how you can find peace, joy, and strength in something that you are waiting on today. Perhaps you simply need to turn your attention to the Lord. Maybe you need to be reminded of the hope of the promise of God. Whatever it is, press in and wait on God. He is faithful to refresh, renew, and restore you.

Faithful One, thank you for your promised strength. When I am weak, you are powerful. When I am disappointed, you are confident and sure. You never waver, and so I look to you—I wait on you—today.

WHOLLY DELIGHTED IN

I am my beloved's,
And his desire is toward me.
SONG OF SOLOMON 7:10 NKJV

When you come to Christ, you are no longer on your own. You belong to him. When you yield your life to his leadership, he welcomes you as friend and beloved. You are not an outsider, a stranger at his table. You are the delight of his heart and the object of his affection. He knows you through and through, and he relishes who you are.

Let all that you do be done from a place of grounded identity. You are wholly loved, wholly accepted, and wholly delighted in. The King of kings and Lord of lords loves you fully, passionately and particularly. Let his love permeate your heart as you allow him to restore your hope, joy, and peace. He pursues you in extravagant love that is pure, true, and strong.

Jesus, thank you for loving me so fully. There isn't anyone else who loves me as wonderfully as you do, and I am overwhelmed by the kindness and goodness of your heart. You always follow through, and I trust you for you are the best friend I have.

AWAKENED TO GRATITUDE

In the middle of the night I awake to give thanks to you
because of all your revelation-light; so right and true!
PSALM 119:62 TPT

Are you tired of waking up in the middle of the night to
worries and situations you can't fix? It would be nice to shut
off our minds, especially when we are prone to overthinking.
That does not mean we are powerless, though.

We get to direct our thoughts and our attention. We don't
have to deny the real worries there, but we also don't have
to dwell on them. The next time you find yourself awake
in the middle of the night with a thought-storm raging
through your head, speak peace to your soul. How? Direct
your thoughts and attention to the Prince of Peace. Think of
things you have and have experienced that you are grateful
for. As you do, thank him for each one. Receive the peace of
his presence that washes over you and find your rest in him.

Lord, thank you for the truth that I am not a victim to my
mind. I get to direct my attention and thoughts, all while
offering you access to my heart. I am so thankful for the
power of your love that meets me and brings peace that
passes understanding.

WITHOUT EXCEPTION

"Love your enemies, do good to them, and lend to them
without expecting to get anything back. Then your reward
will be great, and you will be children of the Most High,
because he is kind to the ungrateful and wicked."

LUKE 6:35 NIV

The law of Christ's love does not put stipulations and
boundaries on it. In fact, the instructions that Christ
gave were to always push us toward giving more love, no
matter the person or situation. We are not only to love our
friends and family, but our actual enemies. He wasn't being
hyperbolic when he said that we should do good to our
enemies, for that is love in action. He meant that we should
actually be kind, lending them what they need and removing
the expectation of receiving anything in return.

Love is not love that gives in order to receive. The love of
God is given freely and generously, and so we are called to
love in the same way. Instead of putting limits on the lengths
we are willing to go in mercy-kindness and compassion, let's
instead push ourselves to stretch the boundaries of our own
love. Let's throw out the excuses we've allowed ourselves to
withhold love from others.

Merciful Jesus, I want to grow in my capacity to love.
Help me to stop making excuses for my biases, hate, and
stinginess. I want to be more like you.

BREAK OF DAWN

"Because of God's tender mercy,
the morning light from heaven is about to break upon us,
to give light to those who sit in darkness
and in the shadow of death,
to guide us to the path of peace."

LUKE 1:78-79 NLT

Wherever you find yourself today, whether full of hope or longing to feel its tendrils wrapping around your heart, know that the mercy of God is near. It is already with you. The dawning of Christ's light that leads us to the paths of peace has already come. You are living in the fullness of his salvation.

If you need a shot of hope today, look to the one who already is closer than your skin. The Spirit reveals the heart of God as we fellowship with him. He opens our understanding and transforms our thoughts in the palpable peace of his presence. No dark night lasts forever. The winter does not draw out in endless measure. Just as the seasons shift and the days cycle, so do our experiences. But God never changes. He is always merciful, always full of peace, and he is always faithful.

Reliable One, transform my heart in your palpable peace today. I want to rest in the lived knowledge that you are with me, and you won't ever fail. Thank you.

WHAT WE KNOW

As He was going along by the Sea of Galilee, He saw Simon and Andrew, the brother of Simon, casting a net in the sea; for they were fishermen. And Jesus said to them, "Follow Me, and I will make you become fishers of people." Immediately they left their nets and followed him.

MARK 1:16-18 NASB

Jesus spoke to people through stories and through metaphors that made sense to the listeners. Jesus did not say to Simon and Andrew "Follow me, and I will make you carpenters of God's kingdom." He took what they already knew and offered them a spiritual incentive. They had been catching fish, but now they were invited to join Jesus and fish for souls.

God is incredibly thoughtful with us. He knows what will speak to our hearts and desires. There is a longing for more in each of our hearts, and he knows this. He calls out to us. He can take our skills and giftings and use them for his kingdom's sake. And this is not a selfish move. It is a partnership and invitation. We receive far more from him than we could ever offer others, yet it becomes our honor to partner with him. He truly is wonderful.

God, thank you for speaking to me personally and in ways that move the strings of my heart. I love you so.

CHALLENGE YOUR HEART

Do everything without grumbling and arguing, so that
you may be blameless and pure, children of God who are
faultless in a crooked and perverted generation, among
whom you shine like stars in the world.

PHILIPPIANS 2:14-15 CSB

Complaining can be an indicator that we have unmet needs
or resentment hiding in our hearts. When you sense yourself
reacting in grumbling or arguing with others when a task is
at hand, consider with curiosity why. You don't have to judge
yourself harshly in order to redirect your actions. You can be
curious with compassion and still choose to act differently.

When you are hesitant to help others, what is the reason?
What comes up? Let it lead you into an open conversation
with your Lord. Do you feel as if others take advantage
of you? Do you think you could spend your time better?
Whatever answers arise, consider how you want to proceed.
You can choose whether to be harsh or soft, closed-off or
open. Keep an open door to the Spirit's voice and allow him
to reveal what is hidden in your heart.

Wise God, you always know what is at work within my
reactions, even when I don't. Help me to see myself as an
ally, not an enemy. Thank you for leadership, agency, and
the ability to change.

BETTER TO BUILD

The wise woman builds her house,
but the foolish pulls it down with her hands.
PROVERBS 14:1 NKJV

When we walk in wisdom, we become builders rather than destroyers. We build our families, our lives, and our communities with encouragement, truth, and love. It is a foolish person that tears down their own lives with the inability to trust, the need to compete with others, and the withholding of love.

Which is better: to be a builder or to be a destroyer? Sure, there are things in this world that certainly need to be dismantled. Broken systems, corrupt companies, and consumerist mentalities tend to be destructive. This verse is speaking to our own lives, though. What are we building with our choices? Who are we building up with our words? We get to choose the lives we live, and only we can do that. We create the worlds we inhabit with our intentions, thoughts, and actions. May we give up the self-destructive cycles that tear down and instead focus on building what we want to see.

Creator, even in the rubble of destruction, you are always building a new thing. You bring life wherever you move. May I partner with your heart and build something that lasts.

CAREFUL RESPONSE

A gentle answer will calm a person's anger,
but an unkind answer will cause more anger.

PROVERBS 15:1 NCV

It is a good practice to be mindful of our responses to others especially in the midst of a high-tension situation. Though we should not expect to do this perfectly, we can still work to manage our responses to others, even when they are combative and not giving the same courtesy.

We all know how to escalate an argument: matching the energy adds fuel to the fire. This is easy to do; in fact, it is natural for most. However, the better way is to ground ourselves and speak the truth in gentleness. This can be like throwing cool water on a fire. Even if it is out of character for you, work on calming yourself before you angrily engage with those on the offensive. If you feel attacked, you don't have to match their energy or choose to join them on the low road. You can instead choose a better way: a more peaceful way for you and for them.

Lord, I need your help in this area. There are so many hot-button topics that set me off these days. I don't want to engage in arguments, but I don't want to back down from the truth. Help me to offer gentle answers when confronted with the anger of others.

TRUTH TELLER

God is not man, that he should lie,
or a son of man, that he should change his mind.
Has he said, and will he not do it?
Or has he spoken, and will he not fulfill it?

NUMBERS 23:19 ESV

Not only does God tell the truth, he is the truth. There isn't a shadow of doubt, manipulation, or deceitfulness in him. God is pure light and love. He is the source of wisdom, power, and strength. He is the most creative being in the universe, and he follows through on his word.

Though you may struggle to believe others when they disappoint you, can you put your total trust in God? What he has said, he will do. What he has spoken, he will fulfill. He promises to be with you to the end of the age. Lean on his wisdom, even and especially when you have reached the end of your own. God is the way, the truth, and the life. Christ is a reliable help, trustworthy leader, and ever-present friend. Look to him in every trial and in every triumph, for he is the same yesterday, today, and forever.

Jesus Christ, thank you for the power of your love that stands the test of time. You do not lie or cheat or steal. You are pure, true, and faithful. I trust you.

PROMISED PEACE

If while we were still enemies, God fully reconciled us to himself through the death of his Son, then something greater than friendship is ours. Now that we are at peace with God, and because we share in his resurrection life, how much more we will be rescued from sin's dominion!

ROMANS 5:10 TPT

One of the greatest promises that God has given to those who come to him is peace of heart, mind, and soul. Anxiety is a common experience in this world. With so much unknown, threats all around, and endless information to swim in, it can be hard to maintain peace.

God does not promise us that we'll never be afraid. But he does promise us his peace that passes understanding through fellowship with him. Even when the storms of life rage, our hearts can dwell in the pervasive peace of his presence. He is the calm that settles our souls. When we are overwhelmed, we have only to look to him and remember he is with us already and we can trust him.

Jesus, thank you for being the Prince of Peace. You don't just offer mercy and hope, but peace that settles my heart in your presence. Thank you.

SAVING GRACE

The grace of God has appeared that offers salvation to all people. It teaches us to say "No" to ungodliness and worldly passions, and to live self-controlled, upright and Godly lives in this present age.

TITUS 2:11-12 NIV

The grace of God is not some weak thing. It is the strength of God, and it is our salvation. He offers us grace upon grace as a gift; we cannot earn it, nor can we lose it. It is always free, always ready for the taking, and always abundant.

With the grace of God at hand, we can choose to say no to the lesser things of this world. We don't have to keep reaching for the next thing when we already have the greatest treasure that we could ever find—peace with God through Christ. We can live lives of integrity where we choose the things that bring life, peace, joy, and love. We can partner with God to build his kingdom in our communities through lives of surrender to his love. He really is good, and it is wonderfully liberating to live by his grace in every area.

Gracious God, I cannot begin to thank you for the bounty of your grace that empowers me to live with intention. Thank you for saving me; thank you for teaching me and guiding me. Thank you for liberating me in your love.

APRIL

Think about the things of heaven,
not the things of earth.

COLOSSIANS 3:2 NLT

IMPOSSIBLE FOR WHOM

"All this may seem impossible to you now, a small remnant of God's people. But is it impossible for me?" says the LORD of Heaven's Armies.

ZECHARIAH 8:6 NLT

It may seem foolish to hope for what God has promised. It may seem improbable according to the way the world is going. Yet, God is able to do far more than we could ever plan or imagine. His ways are perfect, and he does all things well. He accounts for what we could never anticipate. He is always good, and he is always faithful.

We can choose to put our hope in him, relying on his faithfulness and the power of his love to follow through. Nothing is impossible for God. The one who split the seas and who caused the sun to stand still in the sky, the one who calmed storms and heals our diseases, the Creator who put everything into place—this is the one we trust. This is the God we serve. This is the God who we put our hope in for now and forever.

Mighty Creator, there is nothing you cannot do. I trust your wisdom, your timing, and your plan. I trust that you will follow through on every one of your promises. I remember who you are and who I am. You are great.

CHOSEN AND APPOINTED

"You did not choose me but I chose you, and appointed you
that you would go and bear fruit, and that your fruit would
remain, so that whatever you ask of the Father in my name
he may give to you."

JOHN 15:16 NASB

The Lord your God has chosen you and appointed you
to bear the fruit of his kingdom in your life. This is not a
weighty task, but a light one. What an honor we have to
know the power of God's love at work in our lives. As we
yield to his leadership, he fills us with all that he is so that we
become transformed in the light of his nature.

We are transformed by the Spirit's work in us. It is not out
of striving. There is so much grace-strength in the presence
of God when we need his help. He does not despise our
weakness; he offers us his strength when we have none of
our own. Delight in the fact that God has chosen you before
you could even think to choose him. He loves you fiercely
and fully, and he wants nothing but the best for you.

Faithful One, thank you for all that you have done and are
doing in my life. Thank you for what you will continue to
do. Your perfect peace, jubilant joy, refreshing love, constant
kindness, persistent patience, and uplifting hope keep me
coming back to you. I get to choose you because you have
already chosen me.

HE WORKS

From ancient times no one has heard,
no one has listened to,
no eye has seen any God except you
who acts on behalf of the one who waits for him.

ISAIAH 64:4 CSB

God is greater than we can imagine. He does not fit neatly into boxes of our understanding. He does not remain within limits we impose upon him. He dwells in power, truth, and mercy. He cannot be tamed or tied down. He cannot be controlled or manipulated. He delights in partnering with his people, but he loves even more when we step outside the limits of our comfort zones and partner with him.

Waiting upon the Lord is not an inactive time. It requires trust. We continue to do what is ours to do, even if that is simply lying in wait as we pray, hope, and do the work we already have to do. He will not fail us. He is already at work in the details of our lives. He is working in the world, even as we wait.

Mighty God, may my hopes rise to meet who you are, not staying tied down by disappointment or self-protection. Do what only you can do as I continue to wait on you. Thank you, Lord.

PRESSURE IS OFF

"The Helper, the Holy Spirit, whom the Father will send in my name, he will teach you all things, and bring to your remembrance all things that I said to you."

JOHN 14:26 NKJV

We were never meant to carry the weight of perfectionism. While it is good to try our best, redirecting when we see we have gone off course, the fact remains: we are human, and in our humanity, we will falter. The great news is this: we have a holy help in the Spirit of God. He is our greatest helper, teacher, and leader. He fills in the gaps that our minds make, and he brings to remembrance what we have forgotten at just the right time.

We can let the pressure off of ourselves to perform perfectly then, knowing the Holy Spirit will help us when we need him. The Holy Spirit doesn't come and go from us. When we yield to Jesus Christ as our Savior, offering him our hearts and lives, the Spirit makes his home within us. If we are in Christ, we already have access to the Holy Spirit. What wonderful news!

Lord, thank you for your present and sufficient grace, mercy, and kindness. Thank you for your Spirit that dwells within me and guides me with your perfect wisdom. I am so grateful to be known and led by you.

ENTRENCHED IN LOVE

Keep yourselves in the love of God,
waiting for the mercy of our Lord Jesus Christ
that leads to eternal life.

JUDE 1:21 ESV

What does it look like for us to remain in the love of God?
It can be as practical as brushing our teeth each morning
and night, as constant and habitual as making our beds
in the morning and eating throughout the day. It takes
intentionality, but it also takes consistency.

As we clothe ourselves in love each morning, feeding on
the mercy of God throughout our day, we take God's ways
to heart. When we fix our thoughts on the Word of God,
meditating on his nature, we take him into every decision
we make and into every interaction. Let's be sure to fasten
our hearts to the love of God every day, for from Christ we
receive everything we need, including the gift of eternal life.

Everlasting God, thank you for the limitless love you pour
out on us. I want to feast each day on your mercy, receiving
all that I need from your abundant love. Help me to make
the habit of clothing myself in your love every morning.

HEAVENLY HOMELAND

Our homeland is in heaven,
and we are waiting for our Savior, the Lord Jesus Christ,
to come from heaven.

PHILIPPIANS 3:20 NCV

When the world is a mess and we cannot find ourselves at home within it, may we remember the truth that Paul spoke in today's verse: our homeland is in heaven. It is not a copout or a reason to disengage from our lives, but it is a hope that tethers us to a promise that we have yet to know the fullness of.

The hope we have in looking forward to our heavenly home is what John recorded in Revelation 21:3-4: "Now God's presence is with people, and he will live with them. He will wipe away every tear from their eyes, and there will be no more death, sadness, crying, or pain, because the old ways are gone." Though we weep now, one day God will wipe away every tear. Though we grieve now, there will come a day when death is just a memory. In this heavenly homeland, we will thrive in every way. Let's set our hearts and hope on what we await rather than the lack we now know.

Heavenly Father, thank you for the promise of your kingdom coming to earth in fullness. I want to know your presence even now in the waiting. You are my hope, my strength, and my song.

MORE THAN CONQUERORS

Even in the midst of all these things, we triumph over them all, for God has made us to be more than conquerors, and his demonstrated love is our glorious victory over everything.

ROMANS 8:37 TPT

Our greatest victory is not one that we achieved at all but is found in what Christ has already done for us. He has demonstrated the lengths of his love, and the power of his resurrection life has conquered every fear. His love covers our sins, and in Christ we have been completely set free from condemnation and shame.

Knowing that we are liberated in love, we can join with God as partners and confidently live as those who have been redeemed. What mercy we have been shown. Of course we have mercy to extend to others. No circumstance can defeat us, for God has already overcome. We can grow, persist, and trust through everything we go through, for God is our triumph and our holy hope.

Victorious One, there is nothing that you left out of the power of your love when you gave your life, and there is nothing that can escape the triumph of your resurrection life. I am yours, and I come alive in you. Thank you.

LIVES THAT FLOURISH

The righteous will flourish like a palm tree,
they will grow like a cedar of Lebanon.

PSALM 92:12, 14 NIV

We live in a youth-obsessed culture that is constantly giving us tips for how to rewind the clock and erase the evidence of aging. While this may seem appealing to us, there is actually nothing wrong with getting older and embracing the beauty of the process. There are many gifts that come with aging, wisdom being one of the most prized.

As we yield our lives to Christ, living with intentionality, integrity, and openness, we produce the fruit of his kingdom. In fact, the fruit of the Spirit becomes sweeter with time. There is endless wisdom in the Lord. As we fellowship with him, following his lead and adopting his ways of love, the seeds of his mercy continue to bear fruit in our lives. Every life matters, and every person, no matter how young or old, can flourish and thrive in the fields of the King.

Jesus, I want to embrace the gifts that come with getting older instead of trying to resist them. May my life flourish and grow in every harvest season of my life. I trust you.

FREED FROM FEAR

I prayed to the LORD, and he answered me.
He freed me from all my fears.
Those who look to him for help will be radiant with joy.
PSALM 34:4-5 NLT

God really is gracious and good. He is near, he is powerful, and he is concerned with what concerns us. Instead of letting fear overtake our hearts and minds today, let's take that fear to the Father. Let's pray to the Lord and wait for him to answer. David testified that when he prayed to the Lord for help, that God freed him from all his fears. He knew the absolute joy and relief of God's saving grace.

The same grace is available to each of us as we reach out to the Lord today. No fear is too insignificant, and none is too impossible to overcome that God cannot liberate us in the incredible power of his mercy. As we experience God's intervention, we will know the same joy that radiates from a heart that is overwhelmed with awe at how he moves.

Lord, I need your intervention in my life. The fears that threaten to overtake my heart and mind don't give relief, but I know that you do. Answer me in the faithfulness of your love and astound me with your goodness. I rely on you.

TIME TO RISE

A righteous person falls seven times and rises again,
But the wicked stumble in time of disaster.

PROVERBS 24:16 NASB

In the cycles of life, we each can fall into ruts that lead us
away from the kindness of God. That does not mean that we
are out of his reach, however. Knowing that perfection is not
what God expects of us, can we release the need to power
through on our own? Even when we fall, fail, and falter,
God's grace empowers us to rise again.

Is there a harmful cycle that you have been stuck in? Have
you allowed shame to keep you in hiding, or are you ready
to rise in the light of his love? Today is the day to rise up. It
doesn't matter how many times you've regressed or how long
it's been, you can be liberated in the power of God's mercy
once more as you rise up in him. Ask the Spirit for strength
if you lack it. He is your holy help in everything.

Spirit, I don't want to wallow in defeat or failure, and I don't
want to get lost in fear, shame, or hopelessness. As I look to
you, I rise in your mercy. You lift me up. Thank you.

SO MUCH COMPASSION

When he saw the multitudes, he was moved with
compassion for them, because they were weary and
scattered, like sheep having no shepherd.

MATTHEW 9:36 NKJV

As we look at the life of Jesus, we catch glimpses of what
the Father is like, for Christ was and remains the living
expression of God. In all of his interactions with people
in the towns and villages he traveled through while
ministering, Jesus was filled with compassion for them. He
was not indifferent, and he was not judgmental. He was filled
with kindhearted love.

It is important to evaluate what we think of God. Do we
think of him as aloof or as tenderhearted? Do we expect
him to help us while ignoring the needs of others? He is
compassionate toward all. He knows our hearts, he longs to
gather us in as his own, and he sends us out to minister his
heart to all we encounter. Let's open our hearts to him today
and allow his compassion to move us.

Compassionate One, when I consider the incredible
kindness of your heart, I can't help but be humbled by it. I
want to know your love more deeply and to live it out more
consistently. You are beautiful, and so is your compassion.

POWER OF FORGIVENESS

"Judge not, and you will not be judged;
condemn not, and you will not be condemned;
forgive, and you will be forgiven."

LUKE 6:37 ESV

The judgmental will know judgment, and those who condemn others will themselves find that condemnation is also thrown their way. However, those who choose to forgive and to humble themselves will find themselves forgiven. Each of these actions begins, and sometimes remains, in the heart.

This must be something that we focus on in ourselves and not in others. Only we can choose to forgive, and only we can refuse to judge and condemn others. Let your focus remain on what you can do today in your own heart rather than on what others are or aren't doing. What will you choose today?

Father, I don't want to be filled with bitterness or unforgiveness. You see how hard it can be for me to let go, but you are my help, even in this. Release your grace in my heart as I surrender to your love. I want to know the freedom of forgiveness, even as I choose it today. Thank you for your help, your grace, and your patience with me. You are good, so merciful and forgiving.

CLEANSED BY CHRIST

"You are already clean because of the word
I have spoken to you."
JOHN 15:3 CSB

When Jesus described himself as the sprouting vine and his Father as the farmer tending to the branches connected to the vine, he illustrated that he is our source of life, and the Father lifts and prunes us, the branches. The words of Christ are the cleansing power of his life that flows into us.

Jesus continued in verse 4 of John 15, "Abide in me as I abide in you. Just as the branch cannot bear fruit by itself unless it abides in the vine, neither can you unless you abide in me." Christ has cleansed us, and now our duty is to remain in him. We abide in Christ by following his lead, adopting his ways, and staying humble and open to his words. The power of his life reaches us through the Spirit that dwells within. All that we need flows from him, and we bear the fruit of his kingdom as we nourish from his source.

Christ, you are the source of all that I need. I know that as I remain connected to you in life-union with your Spirit that the fruit of your kingdom will grow. Thank you for grafting me into your kingdom and sharing your life with me.

START NOW

Those who wait for perfect weather will never plant seeds;
those who look at every cloud will never harvest crops.
ECCLESIASTES 11:4 NCV

Many of us know the pull of procrastination. If you do,
then you know the feeling of shame and guilt that can also
accompany it. However, the guilt doesn't propel you into
action, it only keeps you stuck in the cycle of putting off
until tomorrow what could be done today. Instead of beating
yourself up for the time wasted, instead approach today as
a clean slate. Today is all you have; you cannot go back, and
you cannot jump forward.

What have you been waiting to start that you can take
practical steps toward today? You don't have to know how
everything will work out, but you can make meaningful
progress as you take it step by step. Plant the seeds, tend to
the work. Even if you just spend twenty minutes working on
something that you have been putting off, do it. There is no
movement without a first step. Keep going. It will pay off.

Lord, I don't want to keep putting things off for tomorrow
when I don't even know how many tomorrows I will have.
Give me grace, wisdom, and persistence as I take steps to
start today.

SWEET AROMAS

Continue to walk surrendered to the extravagant love of Christ, for he surrendered his life as a sacrifice for us. His great love for us was pleasing to God, like an aroma of adoration—a sweet healing fragrance.

EPHESIANS 5:2 TPT

Surrender doesn't sound like an inviting word. Perhaps surrender feels like a total giving up and giving in. Perhaps it brings about images of defeat. When we choose to surrender to the Lord, we gain far more than we could ever give up. The extravagant love of Christ is pure goodness. There is no shadow of shame hidden within it. The love of Christ is powerful, pure, and kind. It is a sweet healing fragrance for all who yield to it.

As we continue to live yielded to the love of God, our lives become aromas of adoration, as well. The sweet fragrance of healing wafts from the lived out love we walk out. There is beauty, healing, and power in our submission to God's ways. His ways are better than ours, and his thoughts are higher than ours. Why would we try to carve our own way when we can follow the paths of peace that lead to his everlasting kingdom?

Lord, I surrender to your love today. May its power infuse every part of me: my heart, my thoughts, my body, my will. I love you.

HEIRS OF THE PROMISE

If you belong to Christ, then you are Abraham's seed,
and heirs according to the promise.

GALATIANS 3:29 NIV

There is no division between the children of God. As Paul
said, "There is neither Jew nor Gentile, neither slave nor free,
nor is there male and female, for you are all one in Christ
Jesus" (Galatians 3:28). There are no class distinctions, no
second-class citizens, in Christ's kingdom. There aren't
some who are more or less like God because of their
gender, birthplace, ethnicity, or any other differentiating
characteristics. If you belong to Christ, you are heirs
according to the promise.

Far be it from any of us to create distinctions in the family of
God. No one is more worthy than another. It doesn't matter
where we live, how we dress, or what our hobbies are. Instead
of creating exclusionary spaces, we should be welcoming
of all. Let's lay down our biases and preferences and treat
everyone with the dignity and respect they find in Christ.

Christ Jesus, help me to be more open and welcoming of
those who are different than me. I want to expand in love, not
shrink in fear or conditioned biases. Help me to throw off the
limitations I put in place that you never do. Thank you.

CONFIDENT ASSURANCE

What should we say about this?
If God is for us, no one can defeat us.
ROMANS 8:31 NCV

If we spend all our energy looking at the problems ahead of us, then we may become overwhelmed by them. If instead we recognize the problems, challenges, and unknowns and then direct our attention to God, we can put them in rightful perspective. We cannot control how things will happen, but we can surely put our trust in the all-powerful one.

God is faithful and he is trustworthy. He can redeem and restore what seems impossibly gone to us. He is able to do far more and far better than we could ever dream. Will we give into despair, or will we rise up in hope? If we are following the ways of God, submitting ourselves to his love and remaining close to his leadership, then we have nothing to fear. If God is for us, who can be against us?

Trustworthy One, there is no one like you. You are faithful, strong, and wise. You see everything clearly; nothing is a mystery to you. I trust you with my life. Have your way, Lord, and strengthen my faith.

TRUST HIM

Seek his will in all you do,
and he will show you which path to take.

PROVERBS 3:6 NLT

God does not withhold his wisdom from those who seek it. He doesn't hide so that no one can find him. He is close, and he is easy to please. When we seek the Lord, becoming intimate with him through fellowship with his Spirit, we are able to follow his leadership more readily. When we know the tone and timbre of his voice, we can recognize it in the busiest of places.

Trust in the Lord completely, join your life to his, and rely on him to guide you in every decision you make. His wisdom is clear, and it always reveals his unchanging nature. Remain humble and open to God's correction and direction, and he will steer you on the paths of his peace. His ways are good, and they are for your good. Know him, love him, and follow him, for you will find yourself loved to life over and over again as you do.

Lord, I trust you to show me which way to go and which decisions to make. Even when your voice is not loud, I know that I can trust your character. Thank you that I get to partner with your purposes as I choose the path ahead of me. I love you.

LIGHT OF LIFE

"I am the Light of the world;
the one who follows me will not walk in the darkness,
but will have the Light of life."

JOHN 8:12 NASB

When we embrace Christ, following him on the path of his laid-down love, we walk in the light of his leadership. All is made clear in his presence. We are not driven by shadows or shame, but by the light of his love.

Where the Spirit of the Lord is, there is freedom. There is not even a thin veil left covering the understanding of our hearts as we turn to the Lord. He is pure light and life, and in him we come alive. He shines on us, and we receive the light of revelation. So, then, let us be sure to look to Christ today, to follow him with our hearts, actions, and lives. As we do, we are covered in the light of his glorious goodness.

Light of the World, I look to you today for understanding, for hope, and for direction. You are the one who fills me up when I am empty. I need you, Lord. Shine on me.

NO MORE WALLS

He himself is our peace, who has made us both one and has broken down in his flesh the dividing wall of hostility.

EPHESIANS 2:14 ESV

In a world filled with chaos, uncertainty, and hostility, where do we find our peace? Though we long for peace in this world, there is a true and lasting peace we have access to right now in the presence of God. Christ is our peace. He has demolished every barrier that stood between us and the Father, and now we are one with him. There is nothing that can separate us from the love of God in Christ.

What is keeping you from experiencing the peace of God in your soul today? Is there fear, shame, or worry? Bring them all to the Lord, casting your burdens before him, for he cares for you. Christ has already removed every barrier, so why would we rebuild them? Instead, let's feast on the peace of his fellowship, for we are his. We can draw near to him, here and now, without fear of rejection.

Prince of Peace, there is nothing that can keep me from your great love. Thank you for the palpable peace I find in your presence. I am yours, and I come to you.

REASON AND SOURCE

We love because he first loved us.

1 JOHN 4:19 CSB

If we are in Christ, having received grace upon grace and love that never ends, there is no excuse for our lack of love toward others. Jesus Christ is our source and our reason. If we love, it is because he loved us first. If we do any good, it is because he has done good to us. He is our standard, as well as our foundation.

If any of us lacks love, we can go to the Lord and receive fresh measures of his mercy today. If any of us doesn't have patience, we can find grace to empower us to endure in God's presence. All that we need is found in fellowship with Christ. Let us do more to love, in all its various expressions, as we ground ourselves in the mercy of Christ. He is our well, and we come to drink from his refreshing springs so that we have something to offer others.

Lord, I know that I have no reason to excuse my lack of love today. I come to you to fill up. Holy Spirit, wash over me with the empowering grace of your presence. I need you. It is my honor to extend the love that I so freely receive from you.

WHATEVER YOU DO

Whether you eat or drink,
or whatever you do,
do all to the glory of God.
1 CORINTHIANS 10:31 NKJV

Everything that we choose and do can reflect the mercy of Christ. We get to live out his love in our lives, aligning with the fruit of his kingdom and the truth of his nature. When we are intentional about the little things, as well as the big things in life, the thread of God's glorious grace weaves through our lives.

How can you focus on glorifying God through your choices today? It may seem silly to you to think about how what you eat can glorify God. In this passage in Corinthians, Paul is speaking about how we can be cognizant of others and try not to offend others over our own personal preferences. With a clear conscience you can eat or drink whatever you want but be sure that you are doing your best to not offend those with differing opinions.

Lord, I recognize that I can take others' views into account as I publicly choose what I will or won't partake of. Help me to be wise and loving, even when my personal preferences don't align with those of others.

RESTORED IN FULL

God is satisfied to have all his fullness dwelling in Christ.
And by the blood of his cross, everything in heaven and
earth is brought back to himself—back to its original intent,
restored to innocence again!

COLOSSIANS 1:19-20 TPT

Christ is the fullness of God in human form. When we look
at the life, ministry, and teachings of Christ, we can know
that they are straight from the heart of God the Father.
Therefore, everything he taught us to prioritize is what God
wants us to prioritize.

Christ's sacrifice is the power of redemption not only for us,
but for everything in creation. We are restored to innocence
in the powerful love of Christ. What he has done can never
be undone, and the threats of darkness cannot overcome the
redemptive power of his resurrection life. Let us find our
hope in him, even as we are revived in the mercy of his heart
that restores us to him completely.

Redeemer, thank you for the power of your restorative
mercy that fills my life. I can't help but be overwhelmed
with awe when I consider that you love me completely and
wholly, and in you I am restored and redeemed. Thank you.

WHOLEHEARTEDLY SEEKING

"You will call on me and come and pray to me,
and I will listen to you.
You will seek me and find me
when you seek me with all your heart."

JEREMIAH 29:12-13 NIV

What we value, we make time for. What we esteem, we make room for. When we love the Lord, let us love him with all our hearts, souls, minds, and strength. Let's give our whole beings to know him, for he has made himself ready to find and easy to please.

When we cultivate hearts that look to the Lord, it becomes almost second nature to turn to him. We can call on him any time, day or night, and come and pray to him. As we continually turn our attention to him, he meets us with the peace of his presence. Knowing God is the greatest venture we can ever take on. And he promises that we will find him, for he is near and he is full of love.

Father, I will pray to you every time I think of you today. In every question, every challenge, and every joy, I will turn my attention to you. Reveal yourself to me as I do. Thank you.

COMPELLED BY COMPASSION

When the Lord saw her,
his heart overflowed with compassion.
"Don't cry!" he said.

LUKE 7:13 NLT

The Lord sees us in our grief, and he is moved with compassion to draw near to us in comfort. He not only sees our pain, but he moves to act on our behalf. In this passage of Scripture, Jesus came upon the funeral of a young man. When Jesus saw the grieving mother, he was quite literally moved with compassion. He went over to the coffin and told the boy to get up. Jesus restored a brokenhearted woman's hope by giving her back her son.

Have you ever experienced the resurrection power of God in your life? Perhaps you had a dream that died, and God resurrected it and gave it back to you. Maybe you have known the power of restored relationship. If you are grieving, know that Christ sees you. He moves to act on your behalf in creative compassion. Trust him.

Restorer, I want to know the power of your compassion at work in my life and the lives of those around me. Move me with your compassion, that I may look for ways to creatively restore hope for the brokenhearted, just as you do.

NOT FINISHED YET

I am confident of this very thing, that he who began a good work among you will complete it by the day of Christ Jesus.

PHILIPPIANS 1:6 NASB

Each of us is a work in progress. If you find yourself discouraged at where you are in life, know this: God is not finished working his mercy out in the details of your story. As Paul said, he who began a good work in you will keep on perfecting it until Christ returns. He is not finished with you, so don't give up hope.

Instead of focusing on the areas of disappointment that can lead to despair, redirect your focus to the keeper of your heart. He who formed the world and all that is in it has not stopped meeting you with mercy. He can take the little you have and build a bounteous and beautiful garden out of it. Will you trust him to do what he has said he will do?

Faithful One, thank you for your persistent mercy in my life and in this world. I believe that you are not finished with me yet; you are my overwhelming hope, and I trust that I will experience your goodness yet in the land of the living.

LOOK FOR THE FRUIT

The fruit of the Spirit is love, joy, peace, patience,
kindness, goodness, faithfulness, gentleness, self-control;
against such things there is no law.

GALATIANS 5:22-23 ESV

It is helpful to know what the fruit of God's kingdom looks,
feels, and tastes like. Otherwise, we could spend our time
drifting in a sea, being tossed back and forth by the winds
of the world, without knowing which direction to go. The
fruit of the Spirit is a compass to us; it reveals where we are
headed.

Looking just under the surface of our actions to the fruit
that is produced by the seeds we plant can reveal our source.
What are the things we rely on? What are the reactions we
are known for? Not only is the fruit of the Spirit something
that is cultivated in our lives as we submit to the Lord and
adopt his ways as our own, but it is also found in the world
around us. The Spirit is working in the world, and we can
see the evidence by the fruit of love, joy, peace, patience,
kindness, goodness, faithfulness, and so on. Let's look for
and follow his fruit.

Spirit, thank you for sowing seeds of peace, goodness, and
joy. The characteristics of how you move are clear to me.
Though I cannot pin you down, I see your fruit and am in
awe of what you do.

FOLLOW HIS LEAD

For the joy that lay before him, he endured the cross,
despising the shame, and sat down at the right hand of the
throne of God.

HEBREWS 12:2 CSB

Jesus is our best example to follow in living humbly, openly, and compassionately. He endured whatever came his way while keeping his attention fixed on the goal at the end of it all. How do we live through difficulties? Do we get bogged down by them, unable to see past our trials? Or do we look to Jesus, the pioneer and perfecter of our faith?

We cannot escape the trials and troubles of life, but we can cling to Jesus as we wade through them. He is our hope, our deliverer, and our joy. He is the fullness of all that we long for and eagerly await. He is our king, and he will never leave us to suffer alone.

Loving Lord, I raise my gaze above the temporary troubles and trials of this life to the eternal glory of your kingdom. You are full of love, and you won't ever keep it from me. Thank you. I choose to follow your lead and keep going, no matter what comes, knowing you are with me through it all.

PREPARING A PLACE

"I am going there to prepare a place for you.
After I go and prepare a place for you,
I will come back and take you to be with me
so that you may be where I am."

JOHN 14:2-3 NCV

Jesus did not abandon us as orphans when he ascended to heaven after his resurrection. He gave us the Holy Spirit to dwell within us, to teach us, and to help us. Though Jesus was one man, the Holy Spirit is not bound by time, space, or body. He is in every believer and moving throughout the earth. He cannot be tamed or tied down.

Even as we have the incomparable goodness of the Holy Spirit with us now, Jesus went to prepare a place for each of us. He promises to return so that we can be with him in body and spirit, with him fully where he dwells. He is actively preparing us for his kingdom, even as he prepares his kingdom for us. What a glorious promise and hope we have in him.

Jesus Christ, I long for the day when I will know the fullness of your kingdom with every sense of my being. I belong to you, and I eagerly await your coming.

WORKS THAT SHINE

"Let your light so shine before men, that they may see your good works and glorify your Father in heaven."

MATTHEW 5:16 NKJV

How we live—how we treat others, the choices we make, and the attitudes we adopt—are ways in which we reveal the values of our hearts. If we truly belong to Christ, following his ways, then our actions will reflect it.

How does your light shine before others? Think through what you are known for: how you interact with strangers and loved ones, what you talk about, what your interests are. What do they say about you? Part of being a child of God is acting like one. This means that we do good to others because he is good to us. We get to be generous with kindness, resources, and hospitality. We are able to forgive others, extending both mercy and grace to others in their imperfections. May we shine bright knowing that our good deeds reflect the love of the Lord.

Holy God, it is because of who you are that I am who I am. Thank you for your mercy, patience, and grace. Help me to never withhold from others what you freely offer me.

MAY

The Spirit God gave us does not
make us timid, but gives us power,
love and self-discipline.

2 TIMOTHY 1:7 NIV

TRUSTWORTHY ONES

You can't trust a gossiper with a secret;
they'll just go blab it all.
Put your confidence instead in a trusted friend,
for he will be faithful to keep it in confidence.
PROVERBS 11:13 TPT

It can be disheartening to realize that you can't trust someone you thought you could, or even that you should be able to trust. This does not mean, however, that there isn't anyone who is trustworthy in your life.

There are faithful friends who keep confidences. The ones who have been tested and proven reliable are sources of strength. They can be trusted with who you are. Instead of focusing too much on those who have weak character, instead thank God for those you have in your circle that you can trust. They are a gift from God.

Perfect One, I know that no one is perfect except you, but I am grateful for the true and steadfast ones in my life. The ones that even when they mess up, humble themselves and repair what needs to be mended in the relationship. I'm so grateful for trusted friends.

HOPEFUL PLANS

"For I know the plans I have for you," declares the LORD,
"plans to prosper you and not to harm you,
plans to give you hope and a future."

JEREMIAH 29:11 NIV

When we don't know what tomorrow will bring, it can
be helpful to ground ourselves in the faithfulness of the
Lord. We may not know where we are going or how our
circumstances will turn out, but the Lord does. He sees every
possibility and guides us with his strong right hand. He will
not lead us somewhere where his grace is not. No matter
what, his presence is our light, our strength, and our peace.

The plans of God are not for our harm but for our good.
He promises us a hope and a future. Even when our bodies
fail, it is not the end. Even when we lose loved ones, it is not
an eternal loss. There is so much more that lies beyond this
little life. In Christ's kingdom there is goodness, love, and
life. There is health, hope, and joy. There is more than we can
imagine. Let's trust him to guide us into his goodness.

Lord, I'm so glad you know what is ahead, even when I have
no idea. I trust you to guide me in your love and to keep my
heart preserved in your peace. I look to you.

IN EVERY SITUATION

I know how to live on almost nothing or with everything. I have learned the secret of living in every situation, whether it is with a full stomach or empty, with plenty or little. For I can do everything through Christ, who gives me strength.

PHILIPPIANS 4:12-13 NLT

Our circumstances do not always reflect the truth of God's love in our lives. There are hard times, sicknesses, and deaths. There is loss and grief. We cannot escape them, for they are part of the human experience. It isn't our job in life to escape pain. No, but God promises to be with us through every season and every situation.

The secret, as Paul put it, to living through the ups and downs of this life with a heart that continues to hope, is to remain connected to Jesus Christ. His presence offers grace that strengthens us in any and every circumstance. We can press into deeper relationship with the Lord at any moment. No matter how little we have, or how abundant our resources are, the Lord's grace remains generous through it all.

Faithful One, thank you for the fellowship I have with your Spirit in every moment. You are only a breath away, if that, at any time. You are my source of strength and my hope. I rely on you.

STRONG DEFENSE

You have been a stronghold for the helpless,
a stronghold for the poor in his distress,
a refuge from the storm, a shade from the heat;
for the breath of the ruthless
is like a rain storm against a wall.

ISAIAH 25:4 NASB

When the ruthless keep on doggedly raining down their diatribes against the vulnerable, there is always a place of shelter in the Lord. He is a defense for the helpless, for the needy in their distress, and a place of refuge from harsh conditions. He is always standing on behalf of the vulnerable ones.

When you are weak, without any one to come to your rescue, the Lord is already near. He is a place of shelter. His peace is palpable. Look to him, lean on him, and call out to him. He is closer than you realize. And when you see someone in need of help and you can do something about it, be the hands and feet of the Lord and intervene.

Mighty God, there is no one like you in all the earth, who is always on the side of the helpless ones. I don't want to sit idly by when I can partner with your purposes. Open my eyes to how I can love in practical ways and be a safe place for the vulnerable.

VESSELS OF THE SPIRIT

We have not received the spirit of the world, but the Spirit who comes from God, so that we may understand what has been freely given to us by God.

1 CORINTHIANS 2:12 CSB

The Spirit of God is not confined by the systems of this world. He is not held down by bureaucracy or limited by the will of those in power. He does not need to hamper the truth in order to protect himself. God is truth, he is mercy, and he is incorruptible.

When we think about this, that God is unimpressed by shows of power and prestige, what do our hearts reveal about what we value? We don't have to live in fear or seeking to control the narrative when we are rooted and grounded in the truth of God's nature. When we value what he values, and we live how he leads and instructs us to, we have nothing to hide. We can freely offer what we receive, for he is our endless source and strength. His ways are infinitely better than the ways of this world, and not only for us, they are liberation to all.

Lord, deepen my understanding of your character and continue to lead me in your powerful mercy. I choose to follow your ways over the systems of this world, for where they confine, you set us free. Thank you.

UPLIFTING ENCOURAGEMENT

Encourage one another and build one another up,
just as you are doing.
1 THESSALONIANS 5:11 ESV

There is no shortage of criticism to dole out with our inflated perceptions of our own values and the judgments of others' motives. However, this is not the way of Christ's kingdom. Instead of dishing out judgment, what if we turned our energy toward building one another up with encouragement? Encouragement does not equal flattery. It can and should be rooted in the truth, calling us up and out of the limitations of our ways to live as God has called us to: as lights of love, justice, and generosity.

When you find yourself getting frustrated with others today, take a moment to reflect on what it is in you that is being activated. Consider how you can give a gentle response instead of tearing someone down with harsh criticism. Look for a kernel of truth—through the lens of God's compassion and grace—and offer encouragement rather than criticism. It can make all the difference in building your relationships.

Father, I know that you don't belittle me with your correction, and I don't want to act that way with others, either. Give me your perspective and the grace to strengthen me in moments of frustration.

REST ON EVERY SIDE

"Is not the LORD your God with you? And has he not given you rest on every side? For he has given the inhabitants of the land into my hand, and the land is subdued before the LORD and before his people."

1 CHRONICLES 22:18 NKJV

With the Lord's presence with you, you have rest. His presence brings peace of mind, heart, and body. It is palpable. No matter what today holds, the Lord is with you. When you begin to worry, turn your attention to the nearness of his presence. He is not far away; he is as close as your breath.

The peace of God puts our hearts at ease. We are able to come undone and truly rest in his care. The atmosphere of God's presence is his peace. He calms the fears that put us on edge and leads us by still waters that we may be refreshed. He restores our soul as we follow him. He is so very gracious with us.

Good Shepherd, thank you for the rest you offer me, even in the midst of tempests and trials. Your presence brings peace, and I find restoration in you. Thank you.

SHARING WITH OTHERS

Does your life in Christ give you strength? Does his love comfort you? Do we share together in the spirit? Do you have mercy and kindness? If so, make me very happy by having the same thoughts, sharing the same love, and having one mind and purpose.

PHILIPPIANS 2:1-2 NCV

The beauty and strength you find in fellowship with the Lord is not meant for you alone. It is a gift to empower you to offer it to others, as well. We are not meant to live as islands, hoarding what we need while cutting ourselves off from others. We are meant to share with one another, to live in the give-and-take of community. We were made for each other; we need each other.

As we look with gratitude on what the Lord has offered us, we can look for ways to spread that joy with others. Whether we open our homes to our neighbors, offer a helping hand to those in need, or comfort those in grief, we are partnering with the power of Christ's life in us. It is so very worth it, and we are blessed as we choose to open our lives in this way.

Generous One, there is no one more benevolent, thoughtful, and kind than you are. I want to be more like you, so I will choose to partner with your goodness as I look for ways to share with others today.

EMPOWERING STRENGTH

God will never give you the spirit of fear, but the Holy Spirit
who gives you mighty power, love, and self-control.
2 Timothy 1:7 TPT

God does not lead with fear. He does not treat us as a cattle
farmer may, pushing and prodding us to keep us in line. He
leads with love in every way, and his kindness is the force
that he uses to draw us to repentance.

Knowing that God leads with mercy, we can adjust our own
leadership. We don't have to intimidate others into our way.
In fact, trying to break people's will in order to fall in line
is as far as we can get from God's ways. The Spirit of God
empowers us in love, strength, and self-control. It is grace
that makes room for us to rise up to meet his expectations.
May we offer the same grace to those in our lives.

Gracious God, there isn't a day where you put aside your
mercy. You are full of loyal love at all times, and even in
correction and justice, you are still leading with kindness. I
want to be more like you, Lord. Help me to leave space for
others in love rather than trying to manipulate them with fear.

NOT CRUSHED

We are hard pressed on every side, but not crushed;
perplexed, but not in despair.

2 CORINTHIANS 4:8 NIV

When life brings its unavoidable hurdles our way, we are not doomed. Even when the pressures of life bear down on every side, we will not be crushed. Though we may be cast down, we are not conquered by anything but the Lord. He is our overwhelming victory, our Prince of peace, our Defender, and our Savior.

The apostles did not have easy lives. They were given over to death, but they counted it as an honor to allow the power of Jesus' life to be made manifest through their humanity. "So then," Paul said in 2 Corinthians 4:12, "Death is working in us, but life in you." What is breaking you down produces life, and fear cannot shut down what it does not control. Don't despair, rejoice in being able to make room for Christ and his power in your weakness.

Jesus Christ, I trust that I will not be crushed by the pressures that seem to be building around me. You are my peace, my hope, and my strength. I trust in you. Be glorified in my life.

GROWING STRONGER

Let your roots grow down into him, and let your lives be built on him. Then your faith will grow strong in the truth you were taught, and you will overflow with thankfulness.

COLOSSIANS 2:7 NLT

If you want to grow strong in faith, you must remain rooted in the mercy of Christ. Allow your roots to grow deep in his love. How do you do this? By getting to know him, by digging deep in his Word and through prayer and fellowship. Your yielded heart makes room for Christ to come in and do a marvelous work.

You cannot skip the elementary steps of learning. Just as children need different levels of training and information throughout their physical and mental development, so do our hearts and spirits need the primary elements of our faith first. Don't neglect keeping your heart open to the teaching of Christ or the wisdom of his leadership. You'll always be a student in his kingdom, but that will look different, depending on the stage you are in. As you grow strong in faith, you will overflow with gratitude, for the Lord is always near and ready to teach you.

Wise God, thank you for the power of your wisdom at work in my life. I won't neglect the importance of learning your ways, and I won't waste time by comparing where I'm at with others. I trust you, my God, my Shepherd, and my Teacher.

HEARTS OF FLESH

"I will give them one heart, and put a new spirit within them.
And I will remove the heart of stone from their flesh
and give them a heart of flesh."

EZEKIEL 11:19 NASB

When our hearts are hardened against others, we are not
without hope. God does an inner work of transformation by
softening our hearts in his mercy. He gives us hearts of flesh,
that we may feel what he feels and be moved by his Spirit.

When we go about our lives with numb hearts, it can feel as if
nothing can affect us. On the other end of the spectrum, we
may feel as if everything is too much. In the hands of the Lord,
we are able to feel what comes up without being overcome by
it. We are able to move in the love of God without shutting
down in indifference. Love is a force unmatched to compel us,
and it is the best motivator in the world.

Merciful God, I don't want to move numbly through my life.
I want to be open to feel the emotions you have given me.
I want to be curious with them, not harsh or judgmental
toward myself or others. Melt my heart in your love and
make me come alive in you.

AGELESS GRACE

"I will pour out my Spirit on all humanity;
then your sons and your daughters will prophesy,
your old men will have dreams,
and your young men will see visions."

JOEL 2:28 CSB

Both the young and old have a place in the kingdom of God.
No one is disqualified from being used by the Spirit of God.
There are gifts for each of us, and no one is excluded. If you
feel as if you are either behind in life, or past your prime,
know that there is no such thing in Christ's kingdom.

You, yes you, have a purpose and a place in Christ. Your age
or experience has not excluded you. God has poured out his
Spirit on all flesh, and that includes yours. He offers you gifts
that are yours to practice and put to use. He is not stingy
with his goodness or kindness. You have more than you can
imagine in the fellowship of his Spirit.

Holy Spirit, thank you for reaching me as I am, and for
depositing elements of Christ's kingdom into my heart and life.
I am in awe of you, and I am humbled by your nearness. I am
open, Lord, pour out a fresh portion of your presence today.

HEMMED IN BY LOVE

"All that the Father gives me will come to me,
and whoever comes to me I will never cast out."
JOHN 6:37 ESV

Christ never turns away those who come to him. He embraces us with love, and he keeps us firmly rooted in his mercy. He does not cast us away, and he will never lose sight of us. He is our good, good shepherd, and he is our faithful friend.

Lay aside your worries of not getting it right today; no matter what "it" is. Christ doesn't need your perfection; he just wants your willingness. Come to him, and don't delay. You are always met with kindness when you do. Let the power of God's love wash over you as you turn yourself to him and open up as a flower opens up to the sun. Let him nourish you and revive you. He is good, and in him you have a forever home.

King Jesus, I'm so grateful that I can't lose my place in your kingdom. Your love is stronger than death, and it is more powerful than my mistakes. You are forever good, and I won't stop looking to you.

BEYOND UNDERSTANDING

A man's heart plans his way,
but the LORD directs his steps.
PROVERBS 16:9 NKJV

It is good to make plans for tomorrow and to take steps toward the goals you make. However, it is important to know that your plans won't be perfect. You can't anticipate what you don't know, and the future always holds mystery for us.

The Lord, in his goodness, sees everything clearly. Nothing can surprise him. That means that even when it looks like our plans are falling apart, God is able to direct us confidently. Though we may experience disappointment as we let go of what we thought would be seamless, God was never under the impression that it would be perfect. He is able to guide us in wisdom for he is trustworthy, faithful, and true. What a relief this is.

Yahweh, you always account for what I can't see, and for that I am grateful. I give up needing to know every detail of my future and trust you to direct my steps, no matter what comes.

COURAGE TO CONQUER

On the day I called you, you answered me.
You made me strong and brave.
PSALM 138:3 NCV

God is our ready help whenever we call on him. We don't have to wait for the "right time" to reach out to him. Whenever we reach out to him is always the right time. He is faithful and true, and he always comes through. He offers strength for our weakness and courage for our fear. He is so very good and always ready.

Though we may be caught off guard by the troubles of life, God is not. He is able to do far more than we can think of asking. He does not grow weary of our asking for his help, so let's never hesitate to reach out to him. His grace is abundant, and his mercy is never-ending. With that kind of supply, we need never limit our requests for his help. He knows us better than we know ourselves, and he offers us all that we need whenever we need it.

Victorious One, sometimes I need courage to even look to you. But I choose to do that today, as well as every time I feel fear closing in on me. You are so good, Lord, and I don't want to limit what you don't limit.

DO IT FOR THE LORD

Put your heart and soul into every activity you do, as though you are doing it for the Lord himself and not merely for others.
COLOSSIANS 3:23 TPT

When we work tirelessly for others, we can reach a point of burnout. Clues that we have reached this point include bitterness at others for asking for our help, general exhaustion around work and relationships, as well as a lack of desire to engage in activities we normally love. This is not what we are called to. We are called to live in the rhythms of God's ways, which includes actual rest.

As far as our work goes, we can focus on taking ownership of what we do choose, offering our efforts to the Lord rather than to please others. Just a subtle shift of intention can change our perspectives about what we are doing and why we are doing it. We cannot escape what needs to be done today, but we can do it unto the Lord, relying on his grace to strengthen us. We can let go of the rest, knowing we were made for relationship and not just to be productive.

Lord, help me to reorient how I approach work. I want to enjoy it, and also to put limits around it so that I can actually rest. Thank you for your help and your wisdom.

NO USE IN WORRYING

"Do not worry about your life, what you will eat or drink; or about your body, what you will wear. Is not life more than food, and the body more than clothes? Look at the birds of the air; they do not sow or reap or store away in barns, and yet your heavenly Father feeds them. Are you not much more valuable than they? Can any one of you by worrying add a single hour to your life?"

MATTHEW 6:25-27 NIV

God knows our hearts, how we are prone to worry. There are real pressures at work in our lives and in the world around us. But he does not call us to be hindered by worry. He empowers us by his grace to be free in his love. He takes care of us, whether we keep those worries in mind or not.

Instead of letting worry weigh us down, we can embrace what we have today while trusting God to take care of what we cannot control. Knowing that we can't add value to our lives by worry, we experience relief as we choose to trust the Lord. Then we can redirect that energy to experience the peace he promises, while also partnering with his love in our lives.

Jesus, thank you for the reminder that worry is wasted energy. I trust you to take care of what I cannot.

OPPORTUNITIES FOR JOY

When troubles of any kind come your way, consider it an opportunity for great joy. For you know that when your faith is tested, your endurance has a chance to grow.

JAMES 1:2-3 NLT

Every test, every challenge, is an opportunity for greater joy. Though the trials of life bring discomfort, pain, and change, they do not steal what God has for us. Perhaps just a change in perspective when unknown challenges arise in our lives can shift our expectations. No matter what we go through, God is the same good God. He still offers us all we need. He promises to never leave us.

Looking for the silver lining doesn't have to mean that we ignore the harsh realities. We can hold hope while also accepting what comes our way. We don't have to dwell in despair. We can walk through grief and still know that there is more joy to experience. Every breaking is an opportunity for expansion.

Lord, I want to know your joy even in disappointment. Help me to look at the troubles of life as opportunities for growth, for greater joy, and for deeper understanding of who you are and who I am in you. Thank you.

NO FEAR OF SHAME

The LORD God helps me,
therefore, I am not disgraced;
therefore, I have made my face like flint,
and I know that I will not be ashamed.

ISAIAH 50:7 NASB

Holy determination is ours when we are convinced of God's help. When his Spirit empowers us to keep going, even when everything feels as if it is falling apart, we can stand strong and persevere in faith. We don't have to conjure this up; we rely on God for help.

As we follow God, even through the hardest parts of life, we don't need to fear being ashamed. Jesus Christ is the victor and our Savior. He loves us completely and redeems our lives as we submit to him. He is better than we can imagine him being. With courage or in our greatest weakness, let's look to the Lord for help and ask him to embolden our hearts that we may keep going.

Lord God, I believe that you are my help and that the power of your mercy and grace is available even now. Help me, Lord, to rise up in courage and to keep persevering in your love even when it's hard. I need you, and I trust you.

CONTENTMENT IS POWERFUL

Keep your lives free from the love of money.
Be satisfied with what you have; for he himself has said,
"I will never leave you or abandon you."
HEBREWS 13:5 CSB

Consumerism runs rampant in our society. We're constantly being fed messages of upgrades and fixes for the inconveniences of normal life. Though we may have all we need in the moment, it is difficult to dwell in the peace of that when there are messages all around of what more we could have. Though the pull for consumption is real, the satisfaction it offers is temporary.

Every time you feel yourself being pulled toward wanting what is advertised to you today, or you feel the pangs of envy when seeing the beautiful things others have, think of one thing that you are thankful for in your own life. Keep a running list this week, no matter how big or small, and nurture the contentment it brings as you ground yourself in gratitude.

Lord, I don't want to mindlessly consume or reach for what is offered me as the better life. My life is full of goodness: things I prayed for and now live in the reality of. Help me to train my heart and mind to find contentment as I look to your very near presence for satisfaction.

REACHING FOR APPROVAL

Am I now seeking the approval of man, or of God?
Or am I trying to please man?
If I were still trying to please man,
I would not be a servant of Christ.

GALATIANS 1:10 ESV

When we are reaching for the approval of others, we will constantly shift ourselves to fit the image of what they find acceptable. It is a losing battle with a moving target. Instead of trying to fit in with others, what would it look like to be grounded in our identity in Christ and look to please God?

Be honest with yourself today. Whose approval are you really looking for? Don't beat yourself up for wanting to please others if that's what is there. Thank God for the ability to redirect and choose differently today. It may be easier to shift this mindset if you are aware of what you are allowing to influence you. It is okay to put up boundaries around your time, your relationships, and your energy. Spend time in the Word, especially in the gospels, and find what God requires of you. Hint: it's a lighter load than you may anticipate. He is gracious and patient with you.

Worthy Lord, thank you for the patience you have for me. I don't want to wake up one day and realize I wasted my life on what others wanted for me. I want to live in the freedom of your love and please you above all else.

IMPARTERS OF GRACE

Let no corrupt word proceed out of your mouth,
but what is good for necessary edification,
that it may impart grace to the hearers.
EPHESIANS 4:29 NKJV

When we become careless with our words, it is bound to affect our relationships. We can build others up with our words, and we can also inflict harm. We cannot expect perfection from ourselves, but we can certainly take the steps to being more mindful and taking responsibility for the words that we speak.

When we realize that we have hurt others by the carelessness of our words, we should be quick to reconcile and offer our sincere apologies. Let's focus on being imparters of grace, offering encouragement and edification. There is grace for us to receive and grace for us to give offer. If we find ourselves running low, let's turn first to our source and the ultimate help. He is quick to offer what we need in every moment so that we can also offer it to those around us.

Gracious God, thank you for the limitless grace I find in your presence. You are always better than I expect, and I want to live out the reflection of your marvelous mercy in my life. When I find myself tearing others down instead of offering truth that builds, give me grace to change.

DO WHAT YOU LOVE

They do not worry about how short life is,
because God keeps them busy with what they love to do.
ECCLESIASTES 5:20 NCV

We have many opportunities in this life to choose what
we do, who we do it with, and how we interact with the
world around us. Doing what we love, including pursuing
the things we are passionate about, reflects walking in the
gifts that God has given us. Even when we find ourselves in
seasons that looked nothing like we had imagined for our
lives, we can still incorporate the things that bring us life.

Don't overlook the power of refreshing rest that comes with
spending time doing what you love. Do you love to host? Plan
a dinner party. Do you like nature? Go for a hike. Do you like
to build things? Start a project. When your life includes doing
what you love, you will not feel as if you have wasted a thing,
no matter how long or short life turns out to be.

Lord, I don't want to waste my life thinking I have no other
options than those I have been living. You are better than
that, and I know that no matter where my feet are planted
that I can still experience peace, joy, and fulfillment by
doing what you created me to do: the things I love doing.

TAPESTRIES OF GOODNESS

We are convinced that every detail of our lives is continually woven together for good, for we are his lovers who have been called to fulfill his designed purpose.

ROMANS 8:28 TPT

As followers of Christ, we do not rely on our ability to perform well in order to live full and fulfilling lives, full of peace, hope, and joy. Every detail is continually woven by the mercy of God into the incomparably good intentions and plans of God. He uses even what seems completely wasted to bring restoration, redemption, and hope. He really is that good.

Instead of dwelling in regret and shame, we can rise up in humble gratitude and grace, knowing nothing is wasted in God's hands. He loves us to life over and over again. He does not shame us for our mistakes, though he does call us to be people of reconciliation. He liberates us in love so that we can be the image of his gracious kindness in our communities. He offers us all we need, all while bringing new life out of the ashes. What a good God he is.

Good Father, I'm so grateful that you weave your gracious goodness through my life, bringing redemption and restoration. May I be a conduit of your mercy right where I am planted. I love you.

FIRM PLANS

The plans of the LORD stand firm forever,
the purposes of his heart through all generations.
PSALM 33:11 NIV

God's plans don't change, even when ours do. What we imagined in our naïve dreaming does not work out perfectly. We don't afford for the hiccups of life and the unknowns we cannot anticipate. Still, this does not mean that God was ever misleading. The reality of his goodness is often far better than our limited imaginings.

Do we truly trust that God's ways are better than our own? He sees the end from the beginning and everything between. He doesn't miss a detail. We don't see the big picture, but we know the one who does. We can trust him more than we trust our own understanding. He is faithful, true, and full of mercy that never ends.

Faithful One, I trust that your plans are better than anyone else's including my own. You aren't surprised by what surprises me, and for that I am eternally grateful. I trust you to continue to lead me in wisdom, truth, and love. I rely on you, Lord, and I believe that you are good.

HE WORKS WITHIN

God is working in you, giving you the desire and the power
to do what pleases him.

PHILIPPIANS 2:13 NLT

You have heard that God looks at the heart while man
looks at the outer appearance. God is not impressed by how
put-together someone might seem on the outside. He sees
straight to the core of a person. This can feel intimidating
if you don't also know that God works in the heart to
transform you from the inside, out.

Ezekiel 36:26 says, "I will give you a new heart, and I will put
a new spirit in you. I will take out your stony, stubborn heart
and give you a tender, responsive heart." No matter what you
see within your heart today, God is able to transform it with
his Spirit. Yield to him and offer him access. You won't be
sorry you did.

Merciful God, I open my heart to you today. I ask you to
transform me. In the areas that I have grown apathetic and
cold-hearted, give me a heart of compassion. I want to know
you more, and I know that it begins in my heart. I am yours.
Have your way in me.

NO ONE FORGOTTEN

"Are five sparrows not sold for two assaria? And yet not one
of them has gone unnoticed in the sight of God."
LUKE 12:6 NASB

Whether you feel overlooked or you grieve at how others
seem to be, take courage from the Word of the Lord today.
No one is forgotten before God. Even those things we deem
insignificant are accounted for by God. If he cares for the
birds of the air, how much more will he care for you?

The vulnerable and oppressed are not shunned by God.
Their position in life is not representative of what God
thinks about them. This is true for us; whether we have
plenty or are in want, each of us is loved completely by God.
May we learn to live in the reality of God's kingdom truth,
lifting others up when we have the chance and by standing
strong in the love of God in our own lives, no matter our
circumstances. Let us not give up on God, for he never gives
up on us.

Loyal Lord, you are full of wisdom, perspective, and power.
You are not lacking in solutions, nor are you lacking in
grace. I stand upon your Word, your nature, and who you
say I am. I love you.

SUSTAINED

He found him in a desolate land,
in a barren, howling wilderness;
he surrounded him, cared for him,
and protected him as the pupil of his eye.

DEUTERONOMY 32:10 CSB

Even if we never step foot in a physical desert, we each will know an emotional and spiritual one. When the wilderness seasons come, we are not alone. Even in the harshest spiritual climates and the most desolate places, God sustains, shields, and cares for us. Not one of those who look to the Lord for help are abandoned.

May we find our strength in the presence of God. We can cultivate closeness with him through fellowship with his Spirit in every season of the soul. He is as good in the hard times as he is in the joyful ones. He is as faithful in love when we are brokenhearted as he is when we are surrounded by loved ones. He is our sustainer, our shield, our guard, and our caregiver. May we trust him with every step.

Faithful God, I don't want to live under the illusion that life is meant to be easy. I want to know your peace in the chaos and your closeness in the wilderness. Be near, oh God, and sustain me.

PERVASIVE PEACE

"I have said these things to you, that in me you
may have peace. In the world you will have tribulation.
But take heart; I have overcome the world."

JOHN 16:33 ESV

The peace that Christ offers us is not dependent upon the
circumstances of life—not even a little bit. He warned over
and over again that we would suffer in this world. He didn't
want any of his followers to be taken by surprise when it
happened. Christ, our living hope, has overcome the world.
He overcame death when he resurrected from the grave. In
him, we have peace that passes all understanding.

What are the things that upset the peace of your heart?
When troubles come, do you find yourself prone to
questioning whether God is truly good? For everything that
gives you anxiety, offer it to the Lord. Ask him to fill your
body with his pervasive peace. The Spirit of God is near,
and he is able to calm your anxious thoughts. Christ is your
peace. Look to him.

Prince of Peace, thank you for the power of your peace in
my heart, life, and in this world. I don't have to be in a calm
environment, even, to experience it. Flood me with your
peace today and settle my heart in your presence.

SACRIFICE OF PRAISE

By him let us continually offer the sacrifice of praise to God,
that is, the fruit of our lips, giving thanks to his name.
HEBREWS 13:15 NKJV

Through Christ, we can offer a continual sacrifice of praise to
God. We look ahead with hope, knowing his kingdom is our
true home. This life—this one messy, imperfect, beautiful,
and brutal life—is what we have to take hold of. When we
are living in the fullness of Christ's kingdom, every veil lifted
and every question answered, praise will not be a sacrifice.

It is in the choosing to praise God through our suffering,
through our doubt and questions, through sickness, loss,
and heartbreak, that we offer a sacrifice of praise. Whatever
we are going through right here and now, whatever we
have been through, and whatever we will go through, we
can praise through it all. Let's offer him the fruit of our lips
today. He is so blessed by the willingness to praise him as a
sacrifice.

Worthy One, I look past the inconveniences of today and
choose to offer you my heart. I praise you, for I am fearfully
and wonderfully made. I praise you because you are worthy,
and you never change. Receive my sacrifice of praise.

JUNE

A cheerful heart is good medicine,
but a crushed spirit
dries up the bones.

PROVERBS 17:22 NIV

FOREVER TRUE

If we are not faithful, he will still be faithful,
because he must be true to who he is.

2 TIMOTHY 2:13 NCV

Even when we fail miserably, God does not change his ways. His nature is as merciful, faithful, and true as it has been or ever will be. This should bring us great relief. God's faithfulness does not depend on our faithfulness, not even one bit.

What would it look like to let the weight of responsibility lift off our shoulders and trust God to faithfully do what he promised to do? We get to partner with him, yes, and what a marvelous privilege that is. However, God is perfect in ways we can never be, and we are not responsible to do work that is his to do. May we embrace the freedom of his mercy and walk in his light, throwing off shame and fear as we look to the faithful one who never fails.

Great God, I'm so grateful that your faithfulness is not dependent upon my own. You are so much better than I give you credit for, and your love is so much bigger than I can fathom. I trust you, even as I take my eyes off of my own failures and fix them on you, the flawless and faithful one.

GOODNESS IN STORE

Things never discovered or heard of before, things beyond our ability to imagine - these are the many things God has in store for all his lovers.

1 CORINTHIANS 2:9 TPT

Spend time today dreaming about the goodness of God and what it looks like. There is more wisdom, better plans, and things greater than we've ever experienced awaiting those who love him. There are treasures hidden in darkness and incomparable peace in his presence. All the good things you could think up fall short of the fullness of his love.

There is hope in Christ and his kingdom. This is true every day and in every way. There is so much goodness in store. He is far better to us than we can imagine him being. We only know in part, but one day we will see God fully, even as he sees us. May we be emboldened in hope, knowing that God is not finished working his miraculous mercy and redemption in our lives and in this world. And beyond it all, there is far more awaiting us in the fullness of his kingdom realm.

Good God, as I imagine your goodness, broaden my perspective of hope. Let expectation and joy arise as I fix my heart on you. You are incomparably good, and I continue to trust you with my life.

EVERLASTING GOD

"Do you not know?
Have you not heard?
The LORD is the everlasting God,
the Creator of the ends of the earth.
He will not grow tired or weary,
and his understanding no one can fathom."

ISAIAH 40:28 NIV

It is almost too much to comprehend that God is everlasting. He was before the beginning of time. He will continue to be after everything we know, this world and all that is in it, has passed away. He is the source of all life. Everything finds its wholeness in him.

This God who was, who is, and who is to come is the one who watches over you and me. He does not grow tired or weary, as it says in today's Scripture. His understanding is far vaster than our own. Who can know what God knows? May we trust him. May we follow him. May we draw our strength from him. We can throw all our hope onto him, for he is faithful and true.

Everlasting One, when I am feeling overwhelmed by life, I will remember the truth that you are never overwhelmed. You don't get tired of acting out of love. You don't grow weary. I trust you, Lord.

GOOD SHEPHERD

"If a man has a hundred sheep and one of them gets lost, what will he do? Won't he leave the ninety-nine others in the wilderness and go to search for the one that is lost until he finds it?"

LUKE 15:4 NLT

Even if we would not go after the one lost sheep, as Jesus describes in this passage, God always does. Heaven and earth rejoice at the redemption of one lost lamb. No matter how far we wander, we are never out of God's reach. This is incredibly good news for each and every one of us.

If you have found yourself off-track from the love of God, wandering away from his ways, it is never too late to turn around and be swept up by your Good Shepherd. He rejoices over you as his own, and he will not shame you. He is so much better than anyone you've ever known. Receive the grace, the redemption, and the love he pursues you with today.

Good Shepherd, I want to be wrapped up in the embrace of your loving care. Help me, Lord, and bring me to where I am meant to be. You are so kind, patient, and powerful. I love you.

SPIRIT INTERCESSION

The Spirit also helps our weakness; for we do not know what to pray for as we should, but the Spirit himself intercedes for us with groanings too deep for words.

ROMANS 8:26 NASB

When we are at a loss for what to pray for or how to pray, it does not mean we are powerless. It is an opportunity for the Spirit of God to intervene and intercede on our behalf. We don't have to have the right words. The Spirit reads our hearts and prays for us. Even in our prayer lives, we don't have to depend on ourselves. What grace is ours in Christ.

When you find yourself wanting to pray but unable to form words, ask the Holy Spirit to intercede on your behalf. Ask him to read the depths of your soul as an offering to God. You don't have to have any words at all. The Spirit Himself will intercede for you with groanings too deep for words.

Holy Spirit, I invite you to read my heart when I have no understanding of my own feelings or how to pray. You know me through and through. Be my intercessor before the Father and pour out your grace, healing, and mercy upon me as I sit in your presence.

INNER STRENGTH

I pray that he may grant you, according to the riches of his glory, to be strengthened with power in your inner being through his Spirit.

EPHESIANS 3:16 CSB

Inner strength is not found in the resources we may or may not have. It is not in our social status or how much money we make. It isn't in the strength of our relationships or the authority of our jobs. It is found in the riches of God's glory. His gracious Spirit empowers us in our inner worlds, giving us strength to persevere in courage. Inner strength is not in pulling up our own bootstraps, so to speak. It's in leaning on the presence of God with us.

With that in mind, how can you shift your perspective of what constitutes strength? There is no shame in weakness; there is opportunity to experience greater measures of God's grace. May you know the power of the Spirit that empowers you when you have nothing left of your own to give. There is always more in him.

Spirit of God, according to your riches, fill me up. When I am weak, be my strength. I want to know the incomparable goodness and strength of your Spirit working in me. I am yours.

SHARE THE WEIGHT

Bear one another's burdens,
and so fulfill the law of Christ.
GALATIANS 6:2 NKJV

In Christ, we are not isolated people trying our best to get
through life unscathed. We were brought into a family: the
family of God. We are now partners with Christ and his
kingdom ways. We get to live out the reality of his kingdom
in the earth, which is powered by love in all its various forms.

One way to live out the ways of Christ's kingdom is to bear
one another's problems. There is power in community and in
carrying a shared load. We can go further together than we
ever could on our own. Instead of trying to power through
our burdens on our own, let's learn to let trusted people in.
Also, may we not hesitate to help those around us with their
own baggage as we are able to walk together in grace and love.

Gracious God, I know that I wasn't created to carry the
weight of burdens too heavy to bear. Show me how to share
my own problems in healthy ways, while also looking for
ways to help others with theirs. Thank you.

HE SEES IT ALL

God is not unjust so as to overlook your work and the love
that you have shown for his name in serving the saints,
as you still do.

HEBREWS 6:10 ESV

If you ever feel as if your work is overlooked by others, it
can be incredibly discouraging. You may wonder, *What's the
use?* Why continue to do good to others when they simply
seem to take advantage of your willingness to help? No act
of love goes unrewarded, and no movement of goodwill goes
unnoticed. God sees it all.

When you feel yourself going down the road of
discouragement in this area, refocus your attention on your
why. Align your choices with the values you hold dear. You
get to choose how you live, and God takes account of it all.
When you choose to walk in the ways of Christ's love, you
can let go of what others may think, do, or say. Live with
integrity, knowing that your choices reflect the values and
heart of your King, and his opinion is the one that matters
the most.

All-Knowing One, I trust that you don't overlook any
sacrifice I make in your love. I trust you to see, to know, and
to remember. Help me to lift the burden of expectation off
of others and to take ownership of my choices to follow you.
I know you won't let me down.

LET GO A LITTLE

You do not know what will happen tomorrow!
Your life is like a mist. You can see it for a short time,
but then it goes away.

JAMES 4:14 NCV

When we perpetually put off what matters until tomorrow, we may wake up to find that our time has run out. Every day is a gift, and it matters. We cannot say what tomorrow will bring, but we can certainly live every moment of this day with intention. There is room for rest, for relationship, and for all that today affords.

Seizing the day does not mean doing everything. It merely means to evaluate what opportunities are yours, and to live truly, choosing engagement with the things that matter and letting go of what is out of your reach. Take some time to ground yourself in the moment by focusing on how your breath moves in and out of your body. Turn your attention to the presence of God, who is nearer than the air you breathe. You cannot control tomorrow, so let go of the need, and engage with the beauty this day offers.

Lord, I believe that your goodness meets me in this very moment. Help me to not put off the life-giving things for tomorrow and help me to seize your love in every interaction today. Awaken my senses to know your nearness more today.

NOURISHING LOVE

"I love each of you with the same love that the Father loves me. You must continually let my love nourish your hearts."
JOHN 15:9 TPT

What does it mean for us to be nourished by the love of God? We can feast upon it every day, filling up on the nutrients God's love offers us. The love of God offers refreshment, energy, and focus. It is food for our souls, water to our hearts, and sunshine to our senses.

We can never get enough of the love of God, and we shouldn't try to skate by on yesterday's portion. There is always a fresh portion for us. When we feel ourselves in need, let's go to the Lord and receive from his overflowing fountain. It is to our strength when we remain well-nourished by his love. Every time we feel the energy of our love dipping, we can turn to him for more. Let's not hesitate to do it over and over again today.

Loving Lord, your mercy is the source of my life, and I don't want to neglect its power. You are present in love at every moment, and I want to continually be filled. I look to you time and again and open my heart to receive from you.

ALWAYS GOOD

The LORD is good to those whose hope is in him,
to the one who seeks him.
LAMENTATIONS 3:25 NIV

When the storms of this world rage, it can be tempting to question where the goodness of God is in the midst of it. Instead of blaming God, what if we posed it as an open and honest question. Where, God, is your goodness in this tragedy? Where are you now? He welcomes our questions, and he answers our cries.

The Lord's character never changes. When we are full of hope and waning in faith, he remains the same faithful God. He remains full of love, patience, peace, and mercy. He is not shaken, even when the earth is shaking. Let's build our lives upon the bedrock of his nature. It is steadfast and sure through every generation. Let's continue to seek him even as we struggle to see him. He is close, and he will not leave us.

Good God, there is no one like you. You are steadfast in love, and your goodness is sure. I trust you to lead me through the hills and the valleys of this life. Bolster my hope in your presence and give me your peace. I set my hope on you again today.

EXTRAVAGANCE

"He returned home to his father. And while he was still a
long way off, his father saw him coming. Filled with love and
compassion, he ran to his son, embraced him, and kissed him."

LUKE 15:20 NLT

Take some time to read through the entire parable of the
prodigal son today. Look at the choices of the young son and
the attitude of the father. Did the father's love ever waver?
God is a good, good Father. As soon as we turn to make the
journey toward him, he comes running to meet us. He wraps
us up in the garments of his mercy and erases our shame.
He is full of compassion that cannot be tamed. His love is
tenacious and unfiltered. He cannot be stopped.

Wherever you find yourself today, whether still on the
lands of your Father working for his kingdom or turning
back from a jaunt in the wilderness, know that the Father's
love is fierce for you. His compassion is like a rushing river
moving toward you. Allow him to cover you with his robes
of righteousness and believe what he says about you.

Good Father, thank you for not tempering your love. I
want to come alive in the redemption of your complete
compassion today. Cover me in your love and speak your
truth over my identity. I am yours, and I humbly come to
you with an open heart.

ACTIVELY MOVING

The word of God is living and active, and sharper than any two-edged sword, even penetrating as far as the division of soul and spirit, of both joints and marrow, and able to judge the thoughts and intentions of the heart.

HEBREWS 4:12 NASB

In John 1:1, Scriptures reveal that "the Word was with God, and the Word was God." The Word of God, according to John, was Jesus Christ. With this in mind reading through today's verse, what strikes you as especially poignant?

Jesus is living and active, piercing as far as the division of soul and spirit. He is able to judge the thoughts and intentions of the heart. His Spirit moves today as powerfully as it did when he walked the earth, cloaked in his humanity. He can do far more than we can. He is able to reach the depths of our souls, piercing our hearts with his truth. He is not finished working, and he is not powerless to save. Lean on him and allow him to move in the depths of your being. He is faithful to do it.

Word of God, move in my heart where only you can. Cut away the things that don't serve my good or your glory. Shine your light of truth on the shadows of my heart and break the power of shame that hides. I trust you.

IN EVERY WAY

Do everything in love.
1 CORINTHIANS 16:14 CSB

If we are to live according to God's law of love, then we have to let go of the need to qualify who is deserving of it. We can only choose our own actions. We cannot control how others act. When we stop trying to affect others' choices, we can truly take hold of the agency we have over our own lives: our inner and outer worlds. As we yield to the love of God, it expands our understanding and breaks down the walls we put up.

Let your one focus be this: Let all that you do be done in love. Instead of making excuses for why you don't need to be kind to some, choose love in all ways and with everyone. Your love is not dependent on others', but you also have an unlimited supply in the presence of God. Lean into it. Simply do what the Scripture says. At the end of the day, ask the Lord to reveal a deeper understanding of his love as you consider what went well and what was really difficult.

Merciful God, help me to let go of every excuse I have to not show love to others. I can choose to be loving, even when I don't like someone. Thank you for that truth and help me to live it out well.

SIMPLE REQUIREMENTS

He has told you, O man, what is good:
and what does the LORD require of you
but to do justice, and to love kindness,
and to walk humbly with your God?
MICAH 6:8 ESV

Where we often complicate the requirements of God, he always simplifies. Is it easy to act justly? No. Is it a simple concept? Surely. When we align our lives with the ways of God, we cannot ignore his nature and his instructions. When we promote justice with our lives, love kindness, and walk humbly with God and before others, we do what God says is good.

When we recognize areas of our belief systems, our lifestyles, and our relationships that are out of alignment with these things, we can ask God for his help. Instead of doubling down on why we don't need to act the way that God says is good, we can choose to follow on his path of love. Pride keeps us from admitting our weaknesses, while humility keeps us open and able to adapt and transform under the wise leadership of our Lord. Let's choose his ways because they are perfect.

Wise One, I don't want to be defensive about my lack of kindness, justice, and humility. I want to reflect your love really and truly in my life, and I know that means being practical and radical in love.

HUMBLING PERSPECTIVE

When I consider Your heavens, the work of Your fingers,
the moon and the stars, which you have ordained,
what is man that you are mindful of him,
and the son of man that you visit him?

PSALM 8:3-4 NKJV

When was the last time you stood outside on a dark, clear night and simply gazed at the stars above? The longer you look, the more stars you can see. It can be difficult to spot in a city's scope, but get out into the wilderness, and the stars shine bright. Even if you never leave the city, you can discover the wonder of the galaxies through NASA imaging. There have been incredible breakthroughs in picture-taking capabilities in space. The more we discover, the smaller our little world seems.

Consider the heavens, the creative work of God's hands. Go to the places or the images that make you feel your small place in this vast world. Allow the awe of creation to lead you to wonder at how insignificant your life is, yet how completely seen, known, and loved you are by the Creator of all things. Respond as you will and direct your heart to the Lord as you do.

Creator, I am in awe of the wonders of your creation and how small I am in the scope of it all. Thank you for loving me, for listening to me, and for calling me your own.

FOCUS ON TODAY

"Don't worry about tomorrow, because tomorrow will have
its own worries. Each day has enough trouble of its own."
MATTHEW 6:34 NCV

Reading through today's verse, note how it makes you feel.
Do you struggle with worry that is constantly projecting
into the future? Are you consumed with the unknowns you
can't account for? As humans, we want to feel like we are in
control. We want to be able to manage our lives. Still, this
isn't fully possible. We only see in part. We can only know
what we know now.

It isn't a bad thing to plan for tomorrow. However, when
planning turns into bids at control, worry may be at the root.
Try only focusing on today. When you feel anxiety rising in
your heart at future events, bring your thoughts back to the
present moment. You can only do what is yours to do today.
Do your best and let go of the rest. God's got it, and you can
trust him.

Faithful One, help me to let go of the need to know what
tomorrow will bring. I don't want to live with that pressure.
I choose to focus on today, on what I can do here and now. I
love you, and I trust you. I give you my worries, and I leave
them there.

CONTINUALLY MADE NEW

It's time to be made new by every revelation
that's been given to you.
EPHESIANS 4:23 TPT

In Christ, we have been made new, and we are continually
being made new. It's both/and. He has made us new
creations in his redemptive love. Still, we are in the process
of being continually transformed into his image. It is
a life-long venture. We haven't reached the end of our
transformation, and that is beautiful news. We are meant to
continue to learn, grow, and change throughout our lives.

Do you hesitate to change your mind when new information
is presented to you? We aren't meant to view the world in the
same way as a two-year old does as we develop and mature.
As we grow, we are able to see nuance in ways we couldn't.
Our lived experience expands our ability to comprehend what
we once couldn't account for. It is the same in our spiritual
lives. We are on a never-ending journey of transformation.
May we be open and willing to enlarge our understanding as
every new revelation expands our experience.

Wise God, I'm so glad I don't have to be afraid of change.
Your love is an expansive force that keeps enlarging my
understanding of who you are, the power of your mercy, and
the role I get to play in it. Continue to make me new and
transform me in your truth.

USE WHAT YOU HAVE

"Silver or gold I do not have,
but what I do have I give you.
In the name of Jesus Christ of Nazareth, walk."
ACTS 3:6 NIV

You don't need riches or large resources in order to make a meaningful impact in the lives of those around you. If you want to make a difference, whether with individuals or with your community, use what you already have access to.

Take your cues from those who have gone before and lived faithful lives that left an impact on those around them. Look at the examples of those mentioned in Scripture. Consider those you respect and aspire to be like in the world around you now. There is so much encouragement to find in the lived experiences of others. What is more, you have a unique part to play in this world. No one can offer what you do, so don't hesitate to live it out today.

Lord, thank you for this day and for the opportunity to do good. Instead of looking at what I don't have, I open my eyes to what you have already given me. What a wealth I have to give out of. Thank you.

EVERYTHING WE NEED

By his divine power, God has given us everything we need
for living a godly life. We have received all of this by coming
to know him, the one who called us to himself by means of
his marvelous glory and excellence.

2 PETER 1:3 NLT

God gives us everything we need for living a life that pleases
him and reflects his nature in the world. If we feel ill-
equipped to love, he offers us his own. When we don't know
how to keep going, he offers us his grace. Whatever we need,
he has already given us. It's found in his fellowship.

Whenever you come to the end of your own means today,
turn to the Lord. Ask him for what you lack. Take a moment
to receive from his Spirit and then do what is yours to do.
Trust him to cover your efforts. You don't have to be perfect,
just willing. Keep going, seeking restoration when you mess
up and stay humble. All the treasures of God's love are in
Christ, and you have more than enough to cover every area
of your life.

Supplier, thank you for providing everything I need to live
a godly life. Your ways are so much better than the ways
and systems of this world. I humble myself before you. Be
glorified in my life as I continually submit to you.

ALWAYS MORE

Grace, mercy and peace will be with us, from God the Father
and from Jesus Christ, the Son of the Father, in truth and love.

2 JOHN 1:3 NASB

God has not left us with a spirit of fear or of anxiety. He does
not give us reason to fret or worry. He offers us generous
grace, plenty of mercy, and palpable peace. All we need to
do is come to the Father through Jesus and ask him to pour
out his presence over us through his Holy Spirit. We receive
richly from his lavish heart.

When the peace of your heart is challenged, when you feel
low on strength, and when you lack love to offer others, turn
to the Lord. Receive from the overflow of his loving heart.
He always has more to offer in his rich presence. He never
runs dry; he is an abundant source of all that you need.

Abundant God, there is no lack in you, and I will not stop
from coming to you with my need. I rely on your mercy,
grace, and peace more than I can say. Thank you for the
abundance in your love and in your presence. You are my
source of refreshing life.

FREEDOM ALL AROUND

The Lord is the Spirit,
and where the Spirit of the Lord is,
there is freedom.

2 CORINTHIANS 3:17 CSB

Wherever the Spirit of the Lord is, there is freedom. No matter where you are today, no matter what circumstance, if the Lord is with you, so is complete liberty. When you feel backed into a corner, ask the Lord to show you what choices you actually have. He breaks down every barrier that could possibly keep you from his love and offers all you need to walk in the freedom of his Spirit.

The powerful liberty of Christ sets you free on the inside. He gives you space to heal. Psalm 18:19 says, "He brought me out into a broad place; he delivered me, because he delighted in me." Christ's redemption sets your soul in wide-open places where you can heal, grow, and transform. What freedom is yours even now.

Spirit of God, thank you for bringing refreshing peace, powerful joy, and overwhelming freedom to my heart, soul, and spirit. You are my liberty, and I come alive in you. Where I feel stuck, show me where I have room to move.

POSSIBILITIES OF GRATITUDE

Give thanks in all circumstances;
for this is the will of God in Christ Jesus for you.
1 Thessalonians 5:18 esv

Gratitude primes our hearts and minds to look for the goodness of God in the world around us. Thankfulness helps us to accept what is, while also holding hope for the possibilities of the not yet. There are a multitude of benefits to practicing gratitude, not the least of which is the peace, joy, and hope that grow as we do.

Habits are powerful. What we put our efforts toward yields results. Why not make gratitude a practice in our daily lives and see what it does for our hearts and thought lives? When we are frustrated, we can still look for reasons to give thanks. When we are overwhelmed, there is still reason to be grateful. What a powerful and personal habit this can be. It can truly change the way we live into each and every day.

Wonderful One, thank you for the air in my lungs and the sun in the sky. Thank you for life, for kindness, and for glimpses of your goodness. I will give thanks in every circumstance I encounter, remembering that you are with me through it all.

LIFEGIVING WISDOM

The excellence of knowledge is that wisdom gives life to those who have it.

ECCLESIASTES 7:12 NKJV

Wisdom is a resource that benefits those who possess it. In another translation, Ecclesiastes 7:12 says, "For wisdom is protection just as money is protection, but the advantage of knowledge is that wisdom keeps its possessors alive" (NASB). Money can protect us by providing means for us to cover our needs. Wisdom is an even greater guard, though, for it cannot waste away, be stolen, or destroyed.

Proverbs 4:7 puts it this way, "Wisdom is the principal thing; Therefore get wisdom. And in all your getting, get understanding." In other words, invest in wisdom with your whole heart. Follow wisdom's ways and leading. We know that Christ is wisdom personified, so we can confidently follow his teachings and know that we are putting first thing's first when we do.

Wise One, I don't want to invest in things that fade away. I want to invest in your wisdom more than I do anything else. I choose to follow you, and not only that, but I choose to cherish you and your leadership in my life. You are the source of every good thing.

RIGHTFUL CONFIDENCE

"If people want to brag, let them brag
that they understand and know me.
Let them brag that I am the LORD,
and that I am kind and fair,
and that I do things that are right on earth.
This kind of bragging pleases me," says the LORD.

JEREMIAH 9:24 NCV

If we want to brag about anything, it should be about the goodness of the Lord. He is kind and fair, and he does what is right. Though we falter, he never does. Though we see in part, he knows everyone and everything through and through. Let's resist the urge to idolize our own opinions, for God is above them all.

It is a trap to believe that we know better than everyone else. Only God is perfect. We are not. Let's remain humble, and if we are tempted to brag, do as the Lord said to Jeremiah. Only the Lord is perfectly righteous. No human can compare. Instead of lifting other people up on pedestals, we must refrain and instead put God on the throne of our hearts and minds. As we do, our hearts will remain in proper perspective.

God, only you are worthy of the esteem of perfection. Keep me from putting others on pedestals that they don't belong on: even myself and my own opinions.

REFRESHING NEWS

"Simply join your life with mine. Learn my ways and you'll discover that I'm gentle, humble, easy to please. You will find refreshment and rest in me."

MATTHEW 11:29 TPT

If the Jesus you know is demanding, easily upset, or completely unrelatable, then you have yet to discover the true Christ. He says himself that when you join your life with his, learning his ways and putting them into practice, that you will find that he is gentle, humble, and easy to please. You will find rest for your soul and refreshing for your heart in his presence.

He really is that good, and following him is meant to bring us relief from the pressures of this world. Though we cannot escape trials or the necessary parts of life, as we join our lives to Christ, he lifts the weight of them. We can follow him with pervasive peace as our portion. What a beautiful hope we have in him right here and now. Find rest in his presence today.

Prince of Peace, whenever I catch a glimpse of your kindness, I am struck by how wonderful you are. You are always better than I expect. Meet me today with the peace of your presence and the joy of your love.

POWERFUL BLESSINGS

"The Lord bless you and keep you;
the Lord make his face shine on you and be gracious to you;
the Lord turn his face toward you and give you peace."
NUMBERS 6:24-26 NIV

As you read today's verse, receive it first as a blessing over you. Perhaps put a hand over your heart as you read it over yourself. Allow yourself to receive the blessing fully in your heart. Invite the presence of God to expand your awareness of his nearness.

As you carry this blessing in your heart throughout your day, offer it as a gift for others, as well. When you encounter people who put your patience to the test, remember this blessing and extend it to them, whether or not you speak a word of it. Your gracious intention is enough to change the atmosphere of your own heart and extend the blessing of God toward them. Bless all people you interact with today and thank God that you are able to give because you have so richly received first from him.

Gracious God, thank you for the blessings I receive from knowing you. I won't withhold them from others today but will give out of the overflow of what you already offer me. Thank you.

RELIABLE HELP

This same God who takes care of me will supply all your needs from his glorious riches, which have been given to us in Christ Jesus.

PHILIPPIANS 4:19 NLT

God is a reliable help in every circumstance. He promises to supply our needs out of the abundance of his resources. We can trust him to do it. Instead of getting caught up in the worry of how we will make it through, we can trust God to cover what we are not able to. It is to our benefit to take him at his Word.

In Christ, we have all that we need. In his fellowship, we find grace-strength, mercy, and peace. There is joy, hope, and faith. He promises to help us, so why should we let fear keep us from living out of his sufficient presence? Let's give God all of our anxieties, the stress that threatens to keep us stuck in cycles of burnout, and the unknowns we cannot control. Let's put all our trust and hope in him, for he is faithful.

Trustworthy One, I don't want to live under the constant stress of what-ifs and lack. Help me to be grounded in your faithfulness, your provision, and your wisdom. I know that you will take care of me.

RESCUED FROM DARKNESS

He rescued us from the domain of darkness, and transferred
us to the kingdom of his beloved Son, in whom we have
redemption, the forgiveness of sins.

COLOSSIANS 1:13-14 NASB

Not only has Christ rescued us from the domain of darkness,
but he has made us come alive in the resurrection power of
his victory over death. What God does not hold against us,
may we not hinder ourselves with. Sin is not our master, but
Christ is. He has become our salvation, and we are liberated
in his lavish love.

Romans 6:6 says, "Our old self was crucified with [Christ],
in order that our body of sin might be done away with,
so that we would no longer be slaves to sin." If we are no
longer slaves to sin, we are free to follow the Lord, to make
mistakes, and seek restoration in his love over and over
again. We are children of the Light, so let's live like it.

Christ, thank you for removing the power that sin, fear, and
death had over us and for welcoming into your kingdom of
mercy. I delight in following you, for you are life, peace, and
joy to my soul. May I shine bright and reflect the wonderful
goodness of your kingdom in my life.

EXCEEDING EXPECTATIONS

When Jesus came to the place, he looked up and said to
him, "Zacchaeus, hurry and come down because today it is
necessary for me to stay at your house."

LUKE 19:5 CSB

When Zacchaeus climbed up into the tree to see over the
crowds, he simply wanted to catch a glimpse of Jesus. He did
not expect anything more than that. Yet, Jesus answered the
hunger in his heart with a great honor; he would come to his
house and stay.

Every little movement of your heart toward the Lord is seen
by him. He honors it with more than you ask for or expect.
His presence is the balm he offers, and it is exceedingly
better than you could hope for. Allow the Lord to speak to
your heart today, and when you hear his voice, answer him.
He loves to meet with you in the ordinary places you dwell.

Jesus, thank you for being and doing more than I expect. You
are so gracious with me, and your presence is a relief and joy
in every moment. Come to my home, enter my heart, and
teach me your ways. I love you. You are welcome here.

JULY

Be kind and loving to each other,
and forgive each other just as God
forgave you in Christ.

EPHESIANS 4:32 NCV

SLEEP SOUNDLY

If you lie down, you will not be afraid;
when you lie down, your sleep will be sweet.
PROVERBS 3:24 ESV

God does not promise us a life without troubles. We cannot expect the world around us to be a place of complete peace. In humanity, we all stumble. None of us does this thing called life perfectly. Still, we can know the powerful peace of God in our hearts and bodies, even as tensions rise around us.

You can rest peacefully, without fear, because God cannot be surprised. He will never leave you. Whatever the morning brings with it, God is with you in it. He has grace, mercy, peace, and love to spare. Tonight, when you lay down to sleep, give your worries and fear to God. As many times as it takes, offer them to him. Receive the peace of God that passes understanding and allow yourself to rest under the watchful care of your faithful Father.

Defender, I know that you are with me through every twist and turn of life. I don't have to prepare myself for the unknown, for you will do it. I trust you and I receive your peace that calms my racing thoughts and feelings of anxiety. Help me to rest sweetly as I sleep and to wake up refreshed.

OUT OF CAPTIVITY

He brought them out of darkness and the shadow of death,
and broke their chains in pieces.

PSALM 107:14 NKJV

Even before Jesus resurrected and broke the chains of sin
and death that we could not escape on our own, God led
his people out of captivity. Psalm 107 recounts the ways
in which God delivered his people over and over again.
The wonderful news for us today is that he still delivers his
people out of darkness, shame, and bondage.

Earlier in the psalm it says this: "Let the redeemed of the
Lord say so, whom He has redeemed from the hand of the
enemy. He satisfies the longing soul and fills the hungry soul
with goodness" (verses 2, 9). Can you recall a time when you
felt completely stuck without a way of escape? How did you
get through it? Recognize the areas where God intervened
on your behalf and thank him for his goodness today.

Redeemer, thank you for bringing me out of cycles of sin,
shame, and fear. I'm so grateful you are the one who breaks
chains and sets the captive free. I am free in your love
because of all that you have done. Thank you.

LEVELS OF TRUST

"Whoever can be trusted with a little
can also be trusted with a lot,
and whoever is dishonest with a little
is dishonest with a lot."

LUKE 16:10 NCV

It would be foolish to trust someone with your valuables who has already proven to take advantage of others. However, those who prove that they are reliable with a little can be entrusted with more. This applies to more than our livelihoods; it's important to know who can be trusted with our hearts.

It is not wise to trust everyone in the same measure. We do not know the intentions of strangers, and we should not assume that everyone who is convincing and charismatic is also trustworthy. Reputation matters, and so does getting to know others. We do not need to judge others in order to be wise about who we share certain portions of our lives with. We should do our best to be people who can be trusted, first with a little, and then with more, and also leave room for others to prove their character.

Wise God, thank you for wisdom and discernment that gives chances to all, but also that does not ignore signs of dishonesty. May I be clear-eyed and rooted in love.

OPEN HEARTS

"Those who listen with open hearts will receive more revelation. But those who don't listen with open hearts will lose what little they think they have!"

MARK 4:25 TPT

An open heart that loves to learn will receive more revelation. A closed-off heart, however, cannot grow in understanding. If we refuse to consider other perspectives, we don't listen with open hearts. We don't have to be afraid of a different experience than our own, nor do we need to fear other perspectives. In fact, it is important to our development that we remain receptive and open to learning new things. This is true in life and in spirituality.

God has not given us a spirit of fear. We have the Holy Spirit who gives us mighty power, love, and self-control (2 Timothy 1:7). Children know that they have more to learn. Perhaps this is why Jesus encouraged his followers to be like little children. They are constantly learning, growing, and adapting. Can we not also do the same as we remain humble before the Lord?

Jesus, I want to grow in understanding, and I know that requires a humble and open heart. Help me to let go of fear that keeps my heart closed off to hearing what is necessary for growth. I humble myself before you and others today.

TELL YOUR STORY

Let the redeemed of the LORD tell their story.
PSALM 107:2 NIV

If you are in Christ, you have a story to tell. How has his love transformed your life? How has his wisdom changed the way that you live? Spend some time with the Lord today, asking for the Spirit to show you the power of his powerful mercy in specific areas of your life.

As you recall what God has done for you, think about how you can share this with someone today. You have a unique testimony—in fact, probably many testimonies—of God's goodness in your life. What he has done for you, he can certainly do for others. And he has not finished working in you yet. There is fertile ground in your life today for a new breakthrough. Even as you wait in hope, do as the psalm says and let the redeemed of the Lord tell their story.

Christ Jesus, thank you for the power of your redemption in my life. Spirit, reveal the thread of your mercy in my life and remind me of your power in specific areas of my life. I want to share the incredible power of your love with others today. I am so thankful for all that you have done, all that you are doing, and all that you have yet to do.

GRACIOUS FREEDOM

Sin is no longer your master,
for you no longer live under the requirements of the law.
Instead, you live under the freedom of God's grace.

ROMANS 6:14 NLT

What does it truly mean for us to live under the freedom of God's grace? Think about the possibilities. There are no limits to God's grace, so we don't fear disappointing him. Even when we mess up in major ways, God receives us with love as we humbly come to him. He will not hold our sin against us.

Psalm 103:12 put it this way, "He has removed our sins as far from us as the east is from the west." If our sin and shame is removed from us, as far as we can imagine, then we are free to live as we choose. This is gracious freedom. This is the power of God's grace. We are free to live under the light of God's love without anything hindering us.

Gracious Father, thank you for lifting the weight of sin, fear, and shame that held me back from living fully under your love. I am free in your grace, and I am undone by the power of this light and joyful expansiveness.

SPACE TO CONTEMPLATE

You know this, my beloved brothers and sisters.
Now everyone must be quick to hear, slow to speak,
and slow to anger.

JAMES 1:19 NASB

There are times when we rush to respond before we are truly ready. There is no reason to jump headlong into speaking our minds when our hearts have not had time to truly digest what we have heard. We can honor others by listening to them, and also recognizing that we don't have to have a clear and ready answer in the moment. It is not our job to convince others of their own experience. We can honor them and also give ourselves space to honor our own process.

God is not threatened by us or our thoughts even about him. Can we follow in his footsteps and ground in his love knowing that we can listen to others without having to rush in with our own thoughts or opinions? We will grow in grace, in understanding, and in wisdom as we do.

Wise God, I'm so grateful that your ways are better than the ways of this world. I don't want to be like those who are quick to jump in with their own opinions instead of truly listening to the people around them. Help me to be like you.

CONFIDENCE TO CONTINUE

"When you pass through the waters,
I will be with you,
and the rivers will not overwhelm you.
When you walk through the fire,
you will not be scorched,
and the flame will not burn you."

ISAIAH 43:2 CSB

God's gracious presence is our peace, our guide, and our guard. He will not leave us or forsake us: not when the waters flood, the rivers rage, or the fires burn hot and fast. He promises to be with us through it all. Let's not fear fierce weather or storms. God is with us as much in times of physical stress as he is in times of relative peace.

God is our confidence to keep going. We don't need to shrink back when the winds of testing blow. It does not mean we are headed in the wrong direction. Let us check in with the Spirit of God each and every day, inviting his wisdom to instruct and lead us. His confident presence gives us courage to persevere through hard times. His presence is our comfort and our strength.

Spirit, thank you for being with me every moment of every day. I rely on your leadership, your perspective, and your strength.

LET GOD

It depends not on human will or exertion,
but on God, who has mercy.
ROMANS 9:16 ESV

The New Living Translation says this: "So it is God who decides to show mercy. We can neither choose it nor work for it." If it is God who chooses to show mercy, then we can neither earn it nor lose it. This should be a welcome relief, especially to those of us who are tired of striving for our place. In Christ and his kingdom, we have been given a place; we don't have to strive for a thing.

When we learn to let go of our need to prove ourselves, we can rest in the mercy of God. There is nothing left to prove. He knows us through and through, and he chose to show us mercy as we are even on our worst days. If we give up the urge to make ourselves worthy, then we can simply be free to live in response to God's gracious gift of mercy. Instead of reaching for an unattainable mark today, let's live in the peace that is ours in Christ here and now in this very moment.

Merciful God, I want to give up striving to prove myself to you and others. In you, I am already enough because you love me. You have offered the fullness of your grace, mercy, and salvation already; what else is there to gain?

OBEDIENCE IS BETTER

"Has the LORD as great delight
in burnt offerings and sacrifices,
as in obeying the voice of the LORD?
Behold, to obey is better than sacrifice,
and to heed than the fat of rams."

1 SAMUEL 15:22 NKJV

To obey is better than sacrifice. It is more pleasing to
the Lord that we obey what he says rather than offering
sacrifices. When we hear the Lord, when we know what he
wants but we refuse to do it, he knows. We cannot trick him
by sacrificing what doesn't matter to us. He sees our hearts;
he knows our excuses. We cannot fool him.

When God speaks to us, he wants our obedience to his voice.
He wants us to trust him as a friend and faithful God. His
perspective is pure, and his instruction is for our benefit.
Will we choose to do what he says, or will we make excuses
while offering him things that he did not ask for? Do the
thing that draws you closer to the Lord. Obedience is better
than sacrifice.

Gracious God, I am so grateful for fellowship with you. I
don't want to take it for granted or make excuses for why I
shouldn't do what you've asked me to. Help me to love you
and to love those around me in spirit and in truth.

HE IS NOT BEHIND

The Lord is not slow in doing what he promised—the way some people understand slowness. But God is being patient with you. He does not want anyone to be lost, but he wants all people to change their hearts and lives.

2 PETER 3:9 NCV

If God is not behind in doing what he has promised, you can also take hope that you are not behind in your life. Your timing does not need to look like others'. God's patience is in his promises, and it is also present in every stage of your life. Stop comparing your life with those around you and find hope, peace, and joy in the gifts of God that are already yours, here and now.

God gives us grace to be transformed in his love. Our hearts, minds, and lives are changed by the power of his mercy. This applies as much to the details as it does to the bigger picture. Can we trust that God is still moving, that he isn't finished working miracles of his mercy in us? If we know that he is with us, sowing his love into every area of our lives, then we know we will continue to see the fruit of it.

Lord, thank you for your present grace and mercy that is working out your purposes in the earth and in my life. I take hope in you.

IN LIGHT OF ETERNITY

We view our slight, short-lived troubles in the light of eternity.
We see our difficulties as the substance that produces for us an
eternal, weighty glory far beyond all comparison.

2 CORINTHIANS 4:17 TPT

When we broaden our perspective beyond our current
reality, it can help us to ground in the expansiveness of
Christ's kingdom and his promises. God dwells in the realm
of eternity. He cannot be hemmed in by any barrier: not
time, space, nor any smallness of understanding we project
onto him.

When frustrations arise today, remember that they will not
last. They will pass. When troubles feel overwhelming to
you, do as Paul did: see them as opportunities to persevere
in grace, knowing that they produce an eternal glory. When
this one, short life is over, you will enter into the fullness of
eternity. What a glorious hope this is.

Lord, help me to keep my problems in perspective today,
remembering that you are above them all. You are not fazed
by the things that faze me. I'm so grateful for this.

CAPABLE HANDS

The eternal God is your refuge,
and underneath are the everlasting arms.
DEUTERONOMY 33:27 NIV

When the pressures of life feel as if they are too much to bear, lean back into the everlasting arms of your heavenly Father. He is right there. He will hold you up with his love and he will be your refuge of peace.

You don't have to go it alone in any area of your life today. Whenever you feel overwhelmed, close your eyes for a moment and picture yourself leaning back into God. Imagine his arms under yours, holding you up. If you are especially tired and feeling at a loss, imagine you are seated in his palms. Take soul-rest in him, even as you continue about your day. You are not alone.

Eternal God, I rely on your help today. I lean back into your capable arms and trust you to do what I cannot. Thank you.

COURAGE TO COME

Let us come boldly to the throne of our gracious God.
There we will receive his mercy, and we will find grace
to help us when we need it most.

HEBREWS 4:16 NLT

There is no reason to withhold our whole hearts from God
today. Whatever keeps us from him is not rooted in the
reality of Christ's mercy. We are fully embraced by him
whenever we come to him. This is why we can come boldly
to the throne of grace. Whenever we need mercy, we receive
fresh portions from his presence. When we need his help,
there is grace-strength available.

Whatever ideas hinder us from wholeheartedly and
confidently coming before the Lord are lies. They may be
rooted in shame, fear, or doubt. We can choose to push
through them and come, anyway. We are always met with the
same abundant mercy and grace of our Father. All that we
need is found in him, so let's not hesitate to run to him today.

Merciful Lord, I don't want to keep myself from coming to
you with anything that's on my heart. I know you see me
fully, know me truly, and love me wholly. You are my courage.

THROUGH CHRIST

The Law was given through Moses;
grace and truth were realized through Jesus Christ.

JOHN 1:17 NASB

Jesus himself said that he came to fulfill the Law that was given to Moses. Though grace and truth did not come fully through the Law, but through Christ, it still serves a purpose. In Christ, every measure of the Law was fulfilled and satisfied. His sacrifice was the ultimate satisfaction, and no further sacrifice is needed.

The truth of God's mercy was clearly revealed through the life, ministry, death, and resurrection of Christ. If we want to know what God is truly like, we have no further to look than Christ. His nature is shared through the power of his laid-down-love. His mercy and grace are revealed through the many parables and teachings of Christ. If we long for grace and truth today, let's look to Christ and his example in the gospels.

Christ Jesus, in you is the fullness of grace and truth. I come to you with hunger in my heart to know you more. Minister to me as I spend time in your Word and in your presence.

POWERFUL LOVE

"I give you a new comman: love one another.
Just as I have loved you, you are also to love one another."
JOHN 13:34 CSB

God never requires from us what he does not first offer to us. This is almost too great a truth to comprehend. All that God wants from us, he has already given us. The love we are to live by is ours through Christ. His love is our source. We love because he first loved us. We could spend an eternity reveling in the power and wonder of such a gift—of such a God.

When you feel as if you are running low on grace and love today, turn your heart toward God and receive from his fullness. Ask him to feel you with all you need. Then, out of the overflow of his provision, you can offer what God offered you. It is a never-ending cycle of reliance, and that is a good thing. He never runs dry. He is our ultimate source, and all that he asks of us, he offers us first.

Gracious God, thank you for the power of your love that fuels my own. As I meditate on the truth that all that you require you have already offered, expand my understanding of your goodness. I am in awe of you.

OPEN MINDS

Then he opened their minds
to understand the Scriptures.

LUKE 24:45 ESV

God's Spirit opens our minds to understand the Scriptures. He gives the Word of God to humankind and shows the way he works in the lives of those who look to him. He moves in us to reveal the power and truth of God through expanded understanding. It is as if he turns on a light in a darkened room, and we are able to see what we couldn't before.

When God speaks in ways you don't understand, don't worry. He won't leave you in confusion. If you are truly listening to him with a heart that wants to know him, he will give you revelation of his truth. He will open the eyes of your heart and mind to understand what he is speaking. Often, what he spoke to us before, we forget. But when he reminds us, he unlocks our minds to understand the scope of his wisdom, grace, and truth.

Wise God, give me revelation of the truth of who you are in new and deeper ways today. Reveal what only you can, and connect the dots that I can't see any continuity in. Thank you.

LOOKING FOR THE SAVIOR

Simon and those who were with him searched for him.
When they found him, they said to him,
"Everyone is looking for you."

MARK 1:36-37 NKJV

God does not hide himself where he cannot be found.
Everyone is looking for the truth in some way or another.
Christ, in his goodness, represented the Father to us in many
ways. The fact that he was easily found was one such way.

In Jeremiah 29:13, God says, "You will seek Me and find
Me, when you search for Me with all your heart." Jesus, in
Matthew 7:7-8 also said, "Seek, and you will find; knock, and
it will be opened to you. For everyone who asks receives, and
he who seeks finds." If you are looking for your Savior today,
wondering where he has gone, know that he is not far away.
He is close: closer than you know. Keep seeking, and you will
find him.

Savior, thank you that you do not hide in a far-off place. I
believe that you are close to me, even now. I look for you—
for the fingerprints of your mercy—throughout the details
of my day. I know you are with me.

THE RIGHT THING

"We don't want to upset these tax collectors. So go to the lake and fish. After you catch the first fish, open its mouth and you will find a coin. Take that coin and give it to the tax collectors for you and me."

MATTHEW 17:27 NCV

Jesus knew that if his disciples caught fish without paying taxes on them that the tax collectors would be upset. Jesus did not encourage rebellion or blatant disregard for the law but to do the right thing, trusting God to provide for what they lacked. We can do the same thing today.

When you find yourself wanting to cut corners, ask yourself if it is truly the right thing to do. Jesus always encouraged integrity. With his life, his teachings, and his example, he offered relief from having to live a perfect life while still encouraging his followers to live a right and righteous one that naysayers could not fault. Follow his leading and trust him with the rest.

Jesus, thank you for the power of your wisdom that instructs us how to live. It considers what we often don't, and I trust that you are better than the systems of this world. I want to live in integrity, honoring you and your name in all that I do. Thank you for the strength to do the harder thing when it is the right thing.

DEEPENING FRIENDSHIP

Look at how much encouragement you've found in your
relationship with the Anointed One! You are filled to
overflowing with his comforting love. You have experienced
a deepening friendship with the Holy Spirit and have felt his
tender affection and mercy.

PHILIPPIANS 2:1 TPT

Read through today's verse again. Have you experienced
what Paul describes in fellowship with the Anointed One?
Have you known encouragement, relief, and comfort in his
love? How have you experienced a deepening friendship
with the Holy Spirit?

You were created to fellowship with the Creator. He made
you to know him, as well as to be fully known by him. Love
is the basis of all that he did, does, and will do. Know that
there is an invitation to you today to deepen your friendship
with God through his Holy Spirit. There is more mercy and
tender affection to find in his presence. You will never reach
the ends of it.

Holy Spirit, I want to grow closer to you today. I am so
encouraged by the clear invitation I have in you to know the
Father and the Son. I am overwhelmed by the reality of your
presence in my life. Speak to me, for I make room for you
and am listening for you.

NO NEED TO FEAR

The LORD is my light and my salvation—
whom shall I fear?
The LORD is the stronghold of my life—
of whom shall I be afraid?

PSALM 27:1 NIV

As we walk with the Lord every day, he is our light to guide us along the way. He is the source of our salvation to defend us each step we take. Even when threats arise, we do not have to give into fear. As we continue to follow the leading of the Lord, he surrounds and protects us. He is the stronghold of our very lives.

Knowing that God is with us, why would we choose to run from him? He is our source of perfect peace, of life-giving love, and of overwhelming hope. He is our strong and mighty defender, and he does not grow tired or weak. No matter what we face, God is by our side. Let's stick close, trusting him to do what only he can do and letting his peace invade our hearts, minds, and bodies.

Faithful One, I trust that your light never dims, and your knowledge is never faulty. You are strong to save, and you always will be. I stick close to you, Lord, for you are my help in every season of the soul.

PATIENT CONFIDENCE

If we look forward to something we don't yet have,
we must wait patiently and confidently.
ROMANS 8:25 NLT

One of the necessary truths of life is that there are seasons:
in the natural world, in our emotional lives, as well as in our
spiritual formation. We only see and know in part in this world.
We do not feign to know everything that God knows. And yet,
we have fellowship with the one who doesn't miss a thing.

If we truly trust the unchanging, merciful, and powerful
nature of the Lord, then there is no reason to fear what
tomorrow will bring. He is faithful, and he will faithfully
follow through on all that he has promised. Patience is a good
and necessary attribute to nurture in our character. It helps us
to continue to press on when the waiting grows long. May we
remain confident in our waiting, being patient and holding
on to hope, for the one in whom we hope is unfailing.

Righteous One, I believe that you will follow through on
every promise you have made. Where I am upholding ideals
that don't align with your character or kingdom, bring me
into alignment with your truth. I trust you.

MIGHTY PROTECTOR

The LORD watches over strangers;
He supports the fatherless and the widow,
but he thwarts the way of the wicked.

PSALM 146:9 NASB

God watches over strangers and immigrants. He supports the fatherless and widows. God protects people without means to protect themselves out of the norms that society dictates. With this in mind, we can ask ourselves: do we also care for those God cares for?

God is better than any ruler or any influential leader we have ever known. His motives are pure, and his standards are perfect. When we begin to excuse our own lack of practical love toward our neighbor, whoever they may be, we are not getting closer to the truth of Christ, but further from it. May we find ourselves standing with God in humble obedience, caring for those whom God cares about without any ulterior motives.

Perfect One, I admit my failings when it comes to loving others the way you said we should. Help me, Lord, and transform me in your perfect perspective. I don't want to make any more excuses for why I don't need to care about those you care deeply for.

TIMELY GUIDANCE

Your ears shall hear a word behind you, saying,
"This is the way, walk in it,"
Whenever you turn to the right hand
or whenever you turn to the left."
ISAIAH 30:21 NKJV

The guidance of God is not always obvious to those around us, but his voice directs us as we move. When we know God—his nature, his ways, and the fruit of his Spirit—we can confidently walk ahead in life knowing he will direct us when we need it. Some decisions will come easier than others, but we can trust that God is with us in each and every one.

The most important thing in life is to nurture the friendship you have with God. Those who know him can recognize his voice, even when it is at a whisper. It cuts through the noise of the world around and pierces the heart. Trust him to guide you and walk confidently as you go.

Good God, more than anything else, I want to know you as a close friend. I want to know, not only what you say, but the tone and timbre of your voice. Speak to me and guide me. I love you and I trust you.

SHARE THE GOODNESS

"Go back to your home, and tell all that God has done for you." And off he went, proclaiming throughout the town how much Jesus had done for him.

LUKE 8:39 CSB

When God moves in our lives, he often directs us to return home and share his goodness with others. We are not all called as nomads and chasers of influence. In fact, God inhabits the ordinary parts of our lives in extraordinary ways. As we learn to embrace his power in the simplicity of our lives, we learn to live in the peace and contentedness of his Spirit with us.

When was the last time you shared something wonderful that happened with your loved ones? Are they the ones you go to first with good news, or are they left out of the loop? Whatever goodness you have experienced this year, month, week, or today, share it with those who know you best. What an opportunity for them to rejoice with you and to be encouraged in their own hearts and lives.

Lord, I don't want to chase after fruitless dreams or relationships. May I come home to the gifts you have already given me, cherishing those who know me and sharing my breakthroughs and joys with them. Thank you for this perspective shift today.

A CHOICE

"No one takes it from me, but I lay it down of my own accord. I have authority to lay it down, and I have authority to take it up again. This charge I have received from my Father."

JOHN 10:18 ESV

We are never truly powerless in any circumstance. We can choose how we will go through it. Our inner lives are completely within our own agency. When we live as victims, we give the power of our story to another. When we take agency over the narrative of our lives, we are able to choose how we show up in the world.

Even Jesus was not a victim. Knowing that the plan of the Father was for him to lay down his life, he chose to do it. God doesn't force us to participate in his will. He allows us to partner with him. Is there an area of your life where you have felt completely powerless? Reflect on the choices you do have and how you can take agency over your part. You are not a victim, but an overcomer in Christ.

Lord Jesus, thank you for the reminder that I am not powerless in my life. Though I cannot control what tomorrow will bring, I can choose how and when to open my heart, the work I choose to participate in, and how I show up in the world. Help me to remember this.

STRENGTH TRAINING

You are rich in everything—in faith, in speaking, in knowledge, in truly wanting to help, and in the love you learned from us. In the same way, be strong also in the grace of giving.

2 CORINTHIANS 8:7 NCV

You are probably familiar with the ways you can train your muscles to become stronger through exercise. It takes consistency, practice, and hard work to strengthen your physical muscles. The same is true of your emotional and spiritual muscles.

Did you know that you can strengthen your spiritual muscles in practical ways? Paul lays out some of the strengths of the Corinthian church in today's verse. He also points out an area where they can grow stronger: in the grace of giving. As you practice practical generosity, doing the hard work of following through and being consistent, your giving will grow strong in the grace of God.

Lord, I forget sometimes how practical you are. I don't want to waste away the opportunities I have thinking that my actions (or inaction) don't matter. Help me to be self-disciplined, wise, and gracious in generosity. Thank you.

CHOOSE WELL

Beloved ones, God has called us to live a life of freedom. But don't view this wonderful freedom as an excuse to set up a base of operations in the natural realm. Constantly love each other and be committed to serve one another.

GALATIANS 5:13 TPT

It is true that it we have been set completely and wonderfully free by Christ. What a truth to cherish. Even so, there is so much opportunity for us to use our freedom to love others in practical ways. Serving one another in love is an honor. When we become too focused on our own benefits, overlooking the needs of others, we lose sight of the heart of God that transcends to all.

You have the freedom to choose how you live; that is always true. Paul's encouragement in Galatians is that we don't use our freedom as an excuse to promote ourselves in his life, but to use it to build each other up in love. How will you use your freedom in Christ's powerful love to show love to others today?

Lord, thank you for the freedom I have in you without bounds and without guilt. I come alive in the liberty of your love. May I use my freedom to honor your name and build others up.

LAY DOWN PRIDE

Live in harmony with one another. Do not be proud,
but be willing to associate with people of low position.
Do not be conceited.

ROMANS 12:16 NIV

The more we become truly acquainted with Christ's love,
the less excuses we have to ignore our own actions and their
consequences. It starts in our hearts, with the intentional
humbling of our egos. Though we each have personal
preferences, these preferences are not God's truth. Let's
refrain from judging others and be willing to associate with
all people, no matter their class or how they appear.

Though we will not like everyone, it does not mean that we
cannot still love them. We do ourselves and others a disservice
when we presume to be better than some. We are all different,
but we are the same before God; we are all worthy of love,
honor, and respect. May we not withhold it from anyone, as
surely as we hope that we will receive the same.

Worthy One, when my pride keeps me from loving others
well, change my perspective with your wisdom. I know that
I am no better than anyone else. May I truly live that out,
loving others well, no matter who they are, what they look
like, or where they come from.

READY TO FORGIVE

Be merciful to me, O LORD,
for I am calling on you constantly.
Give me happiness, O LORD,
for I give myself to you.
O LORD, you are so good, so ready to forgive,
so full of unfailing love for all who ask for your help.

PSALM 86:3-5 NLT

God is full of unfailing love and mercy. He is ready to restore those who come to him. He is so very good. We can call on God constantly without fear that he will turn us away. He always welcomes us with open arms. He helps all who call on him for support.

When we receive the mercy of God, we are able to offer that same mercy to others. In Luke 7:47, Jesus said, "I tell you, her sins—and they are many—have been forgiven, so she has shown me much love. But a person who is forgiven little shows only little love." May we be aware of the depths of mercy we have been shown so that we can share it.

Merciful One, your love knows no bounds. Thank you for helping me every time I cry out to you. As you intervene on my behalf, may I expand in your grace, being ready to share it with others when they need it, as well.

DON'T BE ENSNARED

The fear of man brings a snare,
but one who trusts in the LORD will be protected.
PROVERBS 29:25 NASB

When we fully trust in the Lord, we can let go of the fear of man. This does not only mean that we are not threatened by what others may do to us, but also their very opinion of us. Fear and intimidation hold us back, but confidence in the Lord lifts us out of these cycles.

Is there someone's opinion of you that you dare not upset, even for the sake of the truth? Trust the Lord and ask him to free you from the fear of what could be. Join in the prayer of David in Psalm 56, where he said, "In God, whose word I praise, In God I have put my trust; I shall not be afraid. What can mere mortals do to me?" Don't let your trust falter in God, or compromise who you are, only to appease others. That is a trap, but in Christ you are free to live fully as he has created you to be.

Lord, thank you for your steadfast love that fuels my trust. You are better than anyone else, so why would I be intimidated by others? Help me, Lord, to be free from the fear of man. I trust in you.

AUGUST

You were taught to be made new in your hearts, to become a new person. That new person is made to be like God—made to be truly good and holy.

EPHESIANS 4:23 NCV

IMAGE OF THE ALMIGHTY

The Son is the radiance of God's glory and the exact
expression of his nature, sustaining all things by his powerful
word. After making purification for sins, he sat down at the
right hand of the Majesty on high.

HEBREWS 1:3 CSB

Jesus is the living expression of God's true nature. The
Passion Translation says it this way: "The Son is the dazzling
radiance of God's splendor… his mirror image!" The fullness
of God in human form—that is Jesus Christ. If we want
to know God as he is, then we must look to who Christ
revealed him to be.

As followers of Christ, it is our honor to get to know him
more through the Scriptures and through fellowship with
the Holy Spirit. There is always more for us to discover
about God. We have not attained fullness of revelation, and
we won't until we are face-to-face with him in his glorious
kingdom. Even then, we may continue to be awed by his
wonderful nature, bowing down before him with each new
revelation as the elders and saints are recorded doing in the
book of Revelation.

Jesus Christ, I want to know you more today. Reveal the
majesty of your love and truth to my heart and mind today.
I look to you.

LIFT YOUR FOCUS

If then you have been raised with Christ, seek the things that are above, where Christ is, seated at the right hand of God. Set your minds on things that are above, not on things that are on earth.

COLOSSIANS 3:1-2 ESV

Christ's resurrection is also our resurrection. Christ is seated above the realm of this world, enthroned in power, honor, and authority. This is why we look above the trappings of this world to seek his higher perspective. His wisdom applies so acutely to our lives, yet it transcends beyond the limits of our world.

Instead of getting weighed down by the distractions of this world, let's set our hearts, minds, and lives on the things that matter, and the things that last. Whatever produces love, faith, peace, and hope are indicative of the wisdom of Christ's kingdom. As Paul said, "Whatever is true, whatever is honorable, whatever is just, whatever is pure, whatever is lovely, whatever is commendable, if there is any excellence, if there is anything worthy of praise, think about these things" (Philippians 4:8).

Lord Jesus, I don't want to be bogged down by the temporary things of this world that don't truly matter. Help me to keep my focus on you and your ways, on living rightly and on glorifying your name through it all.

SEASONS FOR EVERYTHING

To everything there is a season,
a time for every purpose under heaven.
ECCLESIASTES 3:1 NKJV

Nothing is wasted in the kingdom of Christ, and you are not ahead or behind, no matter how you may feel at this stage in your life. There are seasons of sowing and seasons of reaping. There are dormant times, when it feels as if nothing at all is happening, though there is growth beyond your sightline. There are times of abundance and times of lack.

What if you began to see your season as an invitation to see and experience God in a new way? You cannot speed up or slow down the physical seasons of the natural world. What makes you think you can do it with spiritual seasons? There is beauty and purpose in every season. Instead of waiting to get to the next one, learn to enjoy what your specific season offers you that others do not. Change your perspective, and you can change your experience.

Lord, I recognize that the society I am in does not teach me to embrace the different seasons in meaningful ways. I want to learn the beauty that is hidden within each one. Help me to embrace the lessons, the advantages, and the hope of the season I am in right now.

ENJOY YOURSELF

People ought to enjoy every day of their lives,
no matter how long they live.
ECCLESIASTES 11:8 NCV

If we don't take time to enjoy ourselves through the ordinary days, as well as the extraordinary ones, we will miss out on one of the key elements of life. Though there is a lot of heaviness in the world, there is still so much beauty. In the midst of the responsibilities of life, let's not forget to incorporate the elements that bring us joy.

Think about the way you spend most of your days. Do you only focus on the serious things, or do you take time to rest and have fun? The ways you choose to enjoy your days may look different from others, and that's okay. Don't overlook the little things that bring refreshment and delight to your soul. Take time to enjoy yourself today, even amid the necessary things that need to get done.

Lord, delight comes from you. I believe this. Show me how joyful you are. I want to know you in more in this way. I let go of the need to be serious all the time. Thank you.

INFINITE UNDERSTANDING

How great is our God!
There's absolutely nothing his power cannot accomplish,
and he has infinite understanding of everything.

PSALM 147:5 TPT

Nothing is too insignificant that God does not know it full well. At the same time, nothing is too overwhelming for him. His power can accomplish whatever it likes. From the hand of God, the universe, as well as each of us, were created. The same one who put planets in motion and created the heavens and the earth can do much more than we can imagine.

Has your idea of God become small? Have you limited God to the things that you have experienced, or do you leave room for the power and majesty of his love to work in greater ways? Whether or not you recognize the extent of God's understanding or power, it is larger than life, all the same. Dare to dream bigger with God today. Pray bigger prayers, ask for increased revelation of his majesty, and keep letting the love of God expand your perspective and expectations.

Majestic One, I believe that there is nothing outside of your grasp. I join with the vastness of your love and ask for breakthrough, as well as the greater things that Jesus promised. Thank you.

UNQUENCHABLE LOVE

Many waters cannot quench love;
rivers cannot sweep it away.
If one were to give all the wealth of one's house for love,
it would be utterly scorned.

SONG OF SOLOMON 8:7 NIV

God's love is fierce and strong. It is an unstoppable force that both stands firm and advances in unending measure. All the treasures of this world would be like a speck of dust in comparison to the value of this pure love.

No matter what you are facing today, the rushing river of God's love floods over and through it. You are never without the love of God, and you cannot escape it. Whatever you walk through today, you do it with the power of God's affection and mercy. You have the fullness of God's love as your source, your strength, and your oasis. Feast on his love, for he cares for you. You can't deplete his limitless resources even if you try. So, why not draw more than you dared to before?

Merciful Father, I have only tasted of your love, but it has changed my life. I want to be continually transformed as you flood my awareness with your affection. I am yours, Lord, and I pour back my love on you.

TAKE A BREAK

The apostles returned to Jesus from their ministry tour and told him all they had done and taught. Then Jesus said, "Let's go off by ourselves to a quiet place and rest awhile." He said this because there were so many people coming and going that Jesus and his apostles didn't even have time to eat.

MARK 6:30-31 NLT

From the beginning of creation, God set apart a time to rest. After working to create the world, God took a Sabbath. He used it to enjoy what he had created. When Jesus' followers returned to him after their ministry tour, he invited them to come off to a secluded place to rest awhile. He knew the power of rest for our souls and bodies, just as God did at the beginning.

When was the last time you truly took a break from the responsibilities of life? In the next few weeks, try to schedule all your work, as well as all the things that feel like work, to six days. Choose a day for your Sabbath, where you can retreat from the demands of life and rest, rejuvenate, and restore. You don't have to be completely still to rest. Do the things that refresh your soul, heart, mind, and body.

Creator, I want to take your invitation to rest seriously. Help me to put aside the endless demands of work and family and create a day where I can truly be refreshed each week.

PEOPLE OF HIS PASTURE

Know that the LORD himself is God;
it is he who has made us, and not we ourselves;
we are his people and the sheep of his pasture.

PSALM 100:3 NASB

If the Lord is our God, then we are the people of his pasture. Let's not hesitate to enter his presence with joy. Let's run into his courts with thanksgiving. Psalm 100 is a poetic song of thanksgiving. It is a beautiful place to start when coming to the Lord with an open heart. We have the privilege of coming boldly before the throne of grace. May our souls run with abandon into the presence of God, opening up to the fullness of his Spirit that is already so very near.

We did not create ourselves. We may make choices to refine our lives, our character, and our trajectories in life, but our origin stories begin in the heart and hands of God. He knit us together in our mother's womb, and we are alive because he put time and effort into who we are. If that doesn't make us overflow with gratitude today, may we meditate on it until it does.

Yahweh, I am yours. I am your child. Thank you for making me as I am, and for advising me in my growth. I love you more than I can say.

SPEAKERS OF TRUTH

Putting away lying, speak the truth, each one to his neighbor, because we are members of one another.

EPHESIANS 4:25 CSB

Though we don't owe everyone our opinions, we do have a responsibility to speak the truth. Simply put, when we are honest, leaving room for what we don't know, we give each other the gift of trust.

Think about the people in your life who are known for their integrity. They are trustworthy with secrets, but they are also unwavering with the truth. They do not cut corners or lie about things: neither the trivial nor the important matters in life. Now consider someone you know who you know that cannot be taken at their word. Perhaps they constantly say what they think others want to hear, but they have been proven to be unreliable when it comes to stating the honest truth. Who would you rather share your life and heart with? Who would you rather be?

Lord, I want to be a speaker of the truth, and to be known as a reliable and loving neighbor and friend. I don't want to hide behind false pretenses or insecurity. Help me to stand on truth, and to be reliable and honest.

CHECK YOUR HEART

Let each one test his own work, and then his reason to boast
will be in himself alone and not in his neighbor. For each
will have to bear his own load.

GALATIANS 6:4-5 ESV

When we are overconcerned with the actions and work
of others around us, we can easily overlook our own
responsibilities. We can only truly choose for ourselves. We
can encourage others and offer advice, but we must leave the
work and follow-through to them.

The same is true of our hearts. It is not our job to convict
hearts. That is the Holy Spirit's work to do. If we can leave
that work to God, then we can focus on what is actually ours
to do. If we are concerned, let's first be concerned with the
intentions of our own hearts. Let's not become distracted by
what we see other's faults to be. As Jesus said, "Why do you
see the speck that is in your brother's eye, but do not notice
the log that is in your own eye?" (Matthew 7:30) Test your
own heart before you jump to judgment of others. There is
wisdom in remaining humble before God, others, and in our
own hearts.

Lord, when I am quick to judge how others fail, remind me
that I should first look at my own life. Thank you for your
grounded wisdom.

HE GETS IT

We do not have a high priest who cannot sympathize with
our weaknesses, but was in all points tempted as we are,
yet without sin.

HEBREWS 4:15 NKJV

Jesus walked this earth as a man. He was born into poverty,
grew up with siblings, and spent time in the wilderness
being tempted. He knows full well what the limitations of
humanity are. He also knows the reality of exhaustion, grief,
and disappointment.

How have you been able to relate to Jesus in his humanity?
Have you discovered relief in knowing that he gets what it is
like to be weak? Even in his weakness, he didn't sin. But he
doesn't throw that in our faces. He uses it as our liberation.
He took on the weight of the world, and he overcame it all.
He is our Savior, but he is also our friend. Bring him your
very real problems, for he understands them.

Jesus, sometimes I forget that you were an actual man that
had to deal with hunger, conflict, and temptation. Thank
you for coming to earth to reveal the heart of the Father and
for doing it as a human so that we can relate to you and you
to us. Help me in my weakness today, Jesus, and speak your
wisdom into my circumstances.

GOD'S DESIRE

The LORD wants to show his mercy to you.
He wants to rise and comfort you.
The LORD is a fair God,
and everyone who waits for his help will be happy.

ISAIAH 30:18 NCV

God's desire is for us to know him in the full glory of his love. He wants to show mercy-kindness to us, to rise up on our behalf, and envelope us in his comforting embrace. If you have had any doubts of God's compassion toward you, may those doubts be laid to rest in the reality of his love today.

God is love. That is not just a nice sentiment, but straight out of Scripture (1 John 4). His desire for you is that you be engulfed in his mercy, liberated in his kindness, and comforted by his nearness. You don't have to dress yourself up or get into a better space—either in your mind, your body, or your heart—in order to receive the fullness of his love today. Receive from his generous mercy. He loves you so!

Lord, I want to receive your mercy, to be comforted by your presence, and to be regenerated by your kindness today. Fill me, even as I open up to you afresh right now. Thank you.

TRUE WISDOM

If you consider yourself to be wise and one who understands
the ways of God, advertise it with a beautiful, fruitful life
guided by wisdom's gentleness. Never brag or boast about
what you've done and you'll prove that you're truly wise.

JAMES 3:13 TPT

Wisdom is not displayed in boasting about accomplishments.
It's certainly not found in degrading others. True wisdom
is not only knowing about the ways of God, but also
implementing them in every area of our lives. Gentleness is a
fruit of the Spirit. It is a mark of a humble heart.

We should not be drawn to those who promote themselves at
the expense of others. That is the opposite of God's wisdom.
Let's allow the gentleness of God's wisdom to lead us into
greater expressions of love. When we refrain from boasting,
we leave room for genuine acknowledgment of what God
has done, is doing, and will continue to do as we yield to his
leadership in our lives.

Wise God, forgive me for how I have been impressed by
those with power, prestige, and big egos. I want to emulate
the truth and power of your gentle and humble wisdom that
is not dependent on what others think of me, but considers
the well-being of others, just the same.

UNCONFINED

"I am the LORD, the God of all mankind.
Is anything too hard for me?"
JEREMIAH 32:27 NIV

God is not restricted by anything. He is certainly not intimidated by what is too hard for us to do, or even what we imagine accomplishing. We have to continually allow the majesty of God to expand our understanding of who he is. Nothing is too hard for him. Nothing.

What limits have you put on God because of your own limitations? It is human nature to project our own experience, personalities, strengths, and weaknesses on others. Yet, this does not mean that our projections are based in reality or truth. Instead of limiting what God can do in your life based on your own expectations, raise your expectations to the power and majesty of who God is. He cannot be contained, and he cannot be controlled by anyone. He is far greater than we could ever give him credit for.

Lord God, I believe that you are better, more powerful, and more righteous than I can imagine. Open my eyes to see you in ways I haven't before. I want to know the power of your loving nature in new measures.

ALONE TIME

After sending them home, he went up into the hills by himself to pray. Night fell while he was there alone.

MATTHEW 14:23 NLT

Jesus knew the importance of alone time. He knew his human limits and spent time alone to pray to his Father and refresh his own heart, energy, and body. Don't feel guilty for needing breaks away from people, even from those you love. They are necessary and good, and can serve to give you renewed love, vision, and energy.

It is also important to incorporate your spirituality and connection to God in times where you can give him your undivided attention. In these times, you can pour out your heart to him and leave space for him to speak to you. Without the need to rush from a place of stillness, you can experience the ease of open conversation and fellowship with him in a one-on-one way. Plan a time of retreat, if only for a couple of hours, and soak in the rest, renewal, and perspective some time away can bring.

Jesus, thank you for your example in the way you lived. I don't want to become so over-stimulated by others that I don't know how to be alone with myself or with you. Refresh me in times of retreat, Lord.

CREATING CONTENTMENT

Not that I speak from need, for I have learned to be content
in whatever circumstances I am.

PHILIPPIANS 4:11 NASB

Have you ever thought to yourself, "I'll be happy when…"?
How has that worked out for you? When we allow the pull
of what-ifs to keep us disconnected from the present and
endlessly reaching for future possibilities, we train ourselves
to look past the goodness we already possess.

None of us can escape loss, hardship, or suffering in this
life. God does not promise us that we will. However, we can
learn to be content in whatever circumstances we are in
by cultivating gratitude, peace, and a close fellowship with
the Holy Spirit each and every day. Contentment is a heart
posture, not a measure of what we do or do not physically
possess. Look for the goodness, for where the light pours in
each and every day. Moments of joy, of peace, and of love.
Little kindnesses, and great comforts. There is reason to
rejoice today, and by noticing these things, you can create
contentment in your heart.

God, thank you for the power of your presence that never
fades or diminishes. You are fully with me every moment.
That is the greatest gift of all. Thank you.

NEVER TOO LATE

Boaz took Ruth, and she became his wife. And he went in to her, and the LORD gave her conception, and she bore a son. Then the women said to Naomi, "Blessed be the LORD, who has not left you this day without a redeemer, and may his name be renowned in Israel!"

RUTH 4:13-14 ESV

God is a God of restoration. Even when all seems lost in our lives and like our best days are firmly behind us, that is not the end of our story. God is a redeemer. He brings life out of the ashes of our despair, and he causes beauty to grow that both astounds and humbles us.

God has not left you without a redeemer. Christ is your holy help, hope, and friend. He is still sowing mercy into your life that will spring with new life. You won't waste away in despair, for God is with you and he is still writing your story. There is joy ahead, and it will nourish and bless you in ways you could not anticipate. Take heart today as you put your hope in him.

Redeemer, thank you that my best years are not behind me. Though I have had goodness in my life, I know there is even more coming as you produce new fruit out of the ashes of my disappointment. I trust you.

ABSOLUTELY INSEPARABLE

I am persuaded that neither death nor life, nor angels nor
rulers, nor things present nor things to come, nor powers,
nor height nor depth, nor any other created thing will be
able to separate us from the love of God that is in Christ
Jesus our Lord.

ROMANS 8:38-39 CSB

Absolutely nothing can separate us from the love of God.
Christ has bridged every gap there ever was, and there is
no stopping the power of his love in our lives. If we are
convinced that anything we do, where we go, or what is
done to us is able to separate us from God's love, then we are
living under a lie. Nothing—not anything in all creation—is
able to separate us from the love of Christ.

With this in mind, what is keeping you from living in the
fullness of God's love? If nothing can separate you from
it, then allow God's mercy-kindness to sweep over you,
bringing you relief, healing, and comfort. He is better than
the best of men, and he extends the full force of his affection
toward you today.

Christ Jesus, thank you for the power of your love that
overcame everything put in its path. There isn't anything
keeping me from the fullness of your mercy today. Flood me
in your presence and love me to life again.

STRENGTH OF HEART

My flesh and my heart fail;
but God is the strength of my heart and my portion forever.
PSALM 73:26 NKJV

Even when our own hearts and motivations fail us, God does not. We may be full of good intentions at the start of a grand new adventure but find that we fall short as we continue in the drudgery of the messy middle. Even when we are weak beyond belief, our bodies losing strength, God remains the strength of our hearts. He does not change.

In the areas you have run out of strength, offer them to God today. Invite the grace of God's presence in each and every one. Ask for his wisdom, his love, and his power. Even as your own expectations fall apart before your eyes, trust God to build even better things in his goodness and in his faithfulness. May you join with the psalmist in saying, "But God is the strength of my heart and my portion forever."

Powerful God, even when my ideas fail, yours never do. I trust you to sustain me in your powerful love. Be my strength both now and forever. I rely on you.

JOY IS COMING

"You will go out with joy and be led out in peace.
The mountains and hills will burst into song before you,
and all the trees in the fields will clap their hands."

ISAIAH 55:12 NCV

In the preceding verse, the Lord says, "The words I speak…
will not return to me empty. They make the things happen
that I want to happen, and they succeed in doing what I send
them to do." The promises of God bring about our joy and
peace. They are for our good, and they never fail to exalt the
goodness of God's nature.

You can trust God and take him at his Word. What he has
spoken, he will follow through on. God's will surely will be
done on the earth as it is in heaven. We can join our prayers
to his purposes and pray as Jesus taught us to pray. As we do,
let us remember that joy is ours in every breakthrough, and
peace is our permanent portion in Christ.

Faithful One, I believe that you are still working your
promises out in my life and in this earth. You aren't finished
moving in miraculous mercy, and your goodness continues
to be poured out. I trust you, Lord, and I hold onto the hope
that joy is coming.

MESSAGE OF PEACE

The Messiah has come to preach this sweet message of peace to you, the ones who were distant, and to those who are near.
EPHESIANS 2:17 TPT

Christ's message is for everyone, everywhere. The message of his peace—the promise of his salvation—is for all who come to him. There is no hierarchy in the kingdom of God, and there are no outcasts.

As children of God, we are to be promoters of peace. Christ's message of peace has become our own. May we not reserve it for those we feel are more worthy to receive it, for none is more qualified than any other. God's love is the great equalizer. Jesus revealed the equanimity of God's salvation through the parable of the workers in the vineyard (Matthew 20). It doesn't matter who we are or how long we have followed Christ, he offers us the same generous peace with God.

Prince of Peace, I don't want to put limitations on your message that you never put. May I treat everyone with the same kindness that you treat me. Peace with God is for all who come to you, and I am grateful to know it and share your good news with others.

UNIFIED AND DIGNIFIED

Before me was a great multitude that no one could count,
from every nation, tribe, people and language, standing
before the throne and before the Lamb. And they cried out
in a loud voice: "Salvation belongs to our God."

REVELATION 7:9-10 NIV

It is important for us to recognize that every tribe, nation,
language, and people will stand before the throne of God
declaring his glory. There will be representatives from every
ethnicity on earth. There is unity and dignity for all people
in the kingdom of Christ.

Instead of waiting for the fullness of Christ's kingdom to
know this type of unity, let's stretch beyond the borders
of those we are comfortable with and treat all people with
dignity, respect, and love. We can get to know those who
are different from us, for there is far more that we have in
common in our humanity. What an opportunity it is to catch
a glimpse of the glory of God's kingdom when we gather
with those who are different from us.

Great God, I want to know the power and beauty of
knowing you in different expressions, cultures, and
friendships. Help me to broaden my horizons and
experience you in ways I never knew I could.

EVER-PRESENT GOODNESS

I can never escape from your Spirit!
I can never get away from your presence!
If I ride the wings of the morning,
if I dwell by the farthest oceans,
even there your hand will guide me,
and your strength will support me.

PSALM 139:7, 9-10 NLT

The Spirit of God is the fullness of God. The Spirit doesn't lack what Christ embodies. The fact that we can never escape from God's Spirit means that we can never escape his goodness. No matter where on earth we go, or what on earth we do, God's presence is there.

Every moment is an opportunity to lean into the ever-present grace of God. The Spirit strengthens us from the inside out, giving us resolve, peace of mind, and courage to persevere through hardships. Whatever you go through today, the presence of God's Spirit is with you; you cannot escape it. There is help for you, strength for your weakness, and guidance for each step.

Spirit of God, thank you for being so very accessible. I rely on your strength, your grace, and your goodness every single day. Move in my life and give me breakthrough that I've been waiting on. I love you.

SHINING BRIGHT

The path of the righteous is like the light of dawn,
that shines brighter and brighter until the full day.
PROVERBS 4:18 NASB

As we follow Christ on the pathway of his love, we walk in
the light of his goodness. He lights our way, and we shine
brighter and brighter until we come before him in fullness.
Even when our lives feel dull, the light of God's love can
shine brightly still.

May we focus on the one who calls us forward: the Son
of righteousness. He shines brighter than the sun, and we
reflect his light in our lives as we yield to his ways. We can
partner with God's purposes as we choose his love, joy,
peace, patience, and kindness. We can reflect the brightness
of Christ's mercy as we join with his heart and do as he
instructed us to do. As we love God and love others, we
shine like bright stars in the night sky, brighter and brighter
until we join with the sun in the fullness of Christ's kingdom.

Jesus, you are source of light, love, and peace. You are my
hope in every season of the soul. I choose to continue to
follow you. Be glorified in my life and may your love shine
through my life as I live to glorify you.

PEACEFUL HEARTS

"Peace I leave with you. My peace I give to you.
I do not give to you as the world gives.
Don't let your heart be troubled or fearful."
JOHN 14:27 CSB

The peace of God is steadfast and sure. It is not given only to be taken away. Do not let your hearts be troubled, Jesus said, and do not let them be afraid. What threatens the peace of your heart and mind today? Know that you do not have to give into worry or fear. You can rest in the peace of God.

Philippians 4:6-7 says this, "Do not worry about anything, but in everything by prayer and supplication with thanksgiving let your requests be made known to God. And the peace of God, which surpasses all understanding, will guard your hearts and your minds in Christ Jesus." Leave your worries with God in prayer, thanking him for taking care of them, and allow the peace of God to fill your heart and mind as you rest in his faithfulness.

Faithful God, thank you for inviting me to leave my worries and fears with you. I don't want to be weighed down by them, not even a little. I choose to give them to you in prayer, and I leave them there. Fill my heart with your peace and calm my mind in your presence.

EVEN MORE GRACE

He gives more grace. Therefore it says, "God opposes the
proud but gives grace to the humble."
JAMES 4:6 ESV

The humble heart receives grace upon grace. When we
remain open to the Lord's leadership, his correction, and
his help, we grow in the strength of faith. God resists the
proud, not because they aren't worthy of help, but because
they refuse to admit their need of it. When we admit our
weakness, it allows us to make room for God to move in and
offer us greater grace.

Though we cannot control how others may choose, we can
choose for ourselves how we approach God. Whether we
come to him out of humble need or proud defiance is our
own choice. We can be completely confident in who we are
in Christ and still be fully humble and open to correction.
May we know whose we are, and the power of keeping an
open-heart posture before the Lord.

Gracious God, I know that you give grace to the humble, but
you resist the proud. I don't want to miss out on the power
of your love in my life because I think I already know better.
Teach me your ways, Lord, and give me even more grace. I
am open to you.

TREASURES OF DARKNESS

"I will give you the treasures of darkness
and hidden riches of secret places,
that you may know that I, the LORD,
who call you by your name,
am the God of Israel."

ISAIAH 45:3 NKJV

When we walk through the valley of the shadow of death, we have nothing to fear. Even in the darkness, in times of deep sorrow and suffering, there are treasures to be found. Sometimes, we can only see the beauty from the other side. Looking back, we can see where the seeds of mercy sprung to life in new and beautiful ways.

Don't resist times of hardship, thinking that you will never experience peace and joy again. Even when you go through unspeakable pain and your heart is being broken wide open, the mercy of God is close. There are secret riches in the spaces of grief that you will know because you had to trudge through it. Allow God to guide you. He will give you these treasures of darkness, and you will be humbled by the sweetness that came out of what only felt bitter at the time.

Lord, I trust you to do what only you can do and bring life to dead things. In the wreckage of my broken dreams, you are still God, and you are still good. Show me the treasures hidden in secret places where only you and I have gone together.

PROMISE KEEPER

Let us hold firmly to the hope that we have confessed,
because we can trust God to do what he promised.

HEBREWS 10:23 NCV

We can trust God to do what he promised. It's really as simple as that. If we can trust him, then we can also hold firmly to the hope we have in Christ. The power of God's love in our lives is revealed through the grace we find in his presence. God always comes through, and he won't ever stop.

If you could lay aside every worry, anxiety, fear, and doubt today, what would that free you to do? If you can rest in the faithfulness of God, especially in the areas that are out of your control, what does that mean for what you can put your energy toward? May you be encouraged by the faithfulness of God and the power of his promises today. Put your hope in him, for he will do all that he said he will.

Faithful God, I believe that you are the way, the truth, and the life. I believe that you will follow through on every promise you have made. Knowing this, I choose to walk in the freedom of your love and empowering grace today. Thank you.

ACCOMPLISHMENTS

God surveyed all he had made and said, "I love it!" For it
pleased him greatly. Evening gave way to morning— day six.
GENESIS 1:31 TPT

When God was finished creating the world and all that
was in it, he looked over it all. When he took it in, he
couldn't help but be pleased with what he found. He loved
it! May we find the same delight as we look over our own
accomplishments and creative endeavors. It is good to take
some time to survey what we had a hand in creating and to
take pleasure in it. Don't just rush on to the next thing.

Just as God loved what he created, we can also truly delight
in what we worked hard to accomplish. It is not conceited to
recognize that what we carried out is worth our recognition.
Think back to the last time you felt a sense of accomplishment.
What was it? Now ask the Lord to tell you what he thought
about that same accomplishment. Revel in the delight of your
Father as he speaks his thoughts over you today.

Creator, thank you for making me with intention and
creativity. I want to delight in the things I put my hands
to in the same way that you do. Reveal your heart over my
efforts today. Thank you.

SING YOUR GRATITUDE

Let the message of Christ dwell among you richly as you teach and admonish one another with all wisdom through psalms, hymns, and songs from the Spirit, singing to God with gratitude in your hearts.

COLOSSIANS 3:16 NIV

Have you ever wondered why we sing when we gather together in communities of faith? Perhaps it comes naturally to you to worship the Lord through song. Maybe it's just not your thing, but you still respect it. Maybe you resist it altogether.

Scripture is filled with examples of those using music to offer their praise to the Lord. In the Psalms, we find many different expressions and poetic songs that were used in the tabernacle of the Lord. Even Paul writes that we should encourage each other through song. Whether or not you like music, choose to connect with God in this way today. Sing a psalm, a hymn, or a spontaneous song of gratitude. Play worship music as you work. Let your heart be encouraged as you join God's Spirit with yours in song today.

Worthy One, I want to connect with you through music today. Move in my heart as I offer songs to you. I love you.

HONORABLE FAITH

It was by faith that Abraham obeyed when God called him to leave home and go to another land that God would give him as his inheritance. He went without knowing where he was going.

HEBREWS 11:8 NLT

When God called Abraham to leave everything he knew and follow him into the great unknown, Abraham had no idea where he would end up. He didn't have a ten-step plan of how to get from where he was to where he felt like God was calling him to go. He simply obeyed and took the first step. As he was on his way, God directed him.

Have you been putting off making the first move of faith for fear of the unknown? Trust that God will guide you, just as he did with Abraham. He goes with you, and he will direct you as you go. You cannot know every detail. You can't plan for every eventuality. Take the first step of faith and trust that God will be with you and redirect you as needed. There is nothing to fear when you walk with the faithful one.

Good God, I trust you to guide me into your goodness, even though I don't know how things will turn out. Settle my heart with your peace and help me to take the leap of faith that has been building up within me. I trust you.

SEPTEMBER

"A good man out of the good treasure of his heart brings forth good; and an evil man out of the evil treasure of his heart brings forth evil. For out of the abundance of the heart his mouth speaks."

LUKE 6:45 NKJV

REASONS TO TRUST

"Behold, God is my salvation,
I will trust and not be afraid;
for the LORD God is my strength and my song,
and he has become my salvation."

ISAIAH 12:2 NASB

Christ is our salvation. He has done everything needed so that we can freely come to him, experience redemption and forgiveness, and to live liberated in his lavish love. Nothing keeps us from fellowship with God when we come to Christ.

If God is our salvation, then there is no reason to be afraid. He is our strength, our reason to sing, and our hope. He is our help, our gracious comfort, and our defender. Think through your journey with the Lord so far. Where can you see his faithfulness shine through? As you remember what he has already done, may your heart take courage and rest in trust as you incorporate it into faith for today, as well as your bright hope for tomorrow.

Lord, I believe you are completely unfailing in love. Your mercy is powerful to save, and I don't have to earn it even one bit. I am grateful for how you have helped me, and I am convinced that you will continue to. I love you, and I trust you.

LIVING WATER

"Whoever drinks the water I give will never be thirsty.
The water I give will become a spring of water gushing up
inside that person, giving eternal life."

JOHN 4:14 CSB

Jesus offers us the living water that satisfies our souls. It is
water that does not just quench our thirsts, but also produces
gushing fountains of the Holy Spirit within us. We can
experience an inner refreshing at all times because of the life
that Christ infuses in us through the Spirit. It really is good,
and it is available to each of us today.

Come to the presence of God and drink deeply from his
refreshing waters. It will revive your soul. It will give you
clarity, energy, and strength to face whatever comes your
way. The fountain of God's presence is unending, and you
can drink from it at any moment, no matter where you are,
for it is found in the inner depths of your soul where God's
Spirit inhabits those who are yielded to Christ. What a
wonderful gift you have in him in every moment.

Holy Spirit, I don't want to neglect the power of your life in
mine. I tune into your presence that is already close and ask
for you to fill me afresh with the powerful living water you
offer. Thank you.

CORDS OF KINDNESS

"I led them with cords of kindness,
with the bands of love,
and I became to them as one
who eases the yoke on their jaws,
and I bent down to them and fed them."

HOSEA 11:4 ESV

God does not enslave us; this is important to recognize. He leads us with kindness and love. When we are in situations that feel constricting, it is not because he has punished us. He uses what the enemy meant for evil and provides for us still. He is our liberator, but even before we experience breakthrough in certain areas, he eases our burdens and feeds us from his kind hand.

There is so much pain in this world. There is suffering all around. Still, it is not God who causes the suffering. He offers us relief and comfort even in our distress. He is close in kindness, unrelenting in love. He relieves the weight of our problems and meets us in the midst of our messes. He really is that good. We can't escape the trials of this world, but we also cannot escape the power of God's mercy meeting us in the middle of each and every one.

Merciful One, thank you for your unrelenting kindness toward me. I am grateful that even in suffering, you are near, lifting the weight of my burdens. I lean on you, trusting that my breakthrough is coming.

LISTEN FOR IT

"My sheep hear my voice, and I know them,
and they follow me."

JOHN 10:27 NKJV

God wants us to know him. He wants us to recognize his voice, whether we are in chaotic spaces or in the quiet wilderness. Let's cultivate a heart that knows him. How do we do this? We begin by knowing his character. Looking through the Scriptures, we can find who God said that he was. There are common threads of mercy, faithfulness, and justice.

Most importantly, Jesus revealed the nature of the Father. Colossians 1:15 says, "[Christ] is the image of the invisible God, the firstborn over all creation." He is the revelation of God's nature in flesh and blood. Remember, too, that we have the Spirit of God to reveal the ways of God, to fellowship with the Father, and to experience the fruit of his kingdom. As we follow God, spending time with him each day, we grow accustomed to his voice, how he moves, and what he's like.

Good Shepherd, thank you that you are accessible and near today. Speak to me, and bring life, hope, and clarity to my heart and mind as you do. I want to know you more.

HEART DETECTION

"These people show honor to me with words,
but their hearts are far from me."

MARK 7:6 NCV

Jesus knew the hearts of the religious scholars who challenged the way that he and his disciples lived. In the minds of the Pharisees and religious leaders, Jesus' disciples were not following the letter of the law. But Jesus, the Son of God, called them out on their hypocrisy. Though they may have outwardly lived religious lives, their hearts were far from the Lord.

Knowing that God cannot be controlled or manipulated, let's remain humble before him. When he redirects us and corrects our pride, let's be open to admitting where we have been wrong instead of pointing out where others may be missing the mark. 1 Samuel 16:7 reminds us, "God does not see the same way people see. People look at the outside of a person, but the Lord looks at the heart." What does God find as he looks at your heart today?

All-Knowing One, I don't want to be stuck in pride, closed-off to your Word or ways. I humble my heart before you. As David prayed, so do I: cleanse me and I will be clean; wash me, and I will be whiter than snow.

EVERY DETAIL

Tell him every detail of your life, then God's wonderful peace
that transcends human understanding, will guard your heart
and mind through Jesus Christ.

PHILIPPIANS 4:6-7 TPT

You don't have to hide a single detail about your life from
God. He wants in on it all. It's not frivolous to talk to him as
you do a friend. In fact, your fellowship with his Spirit will
grow even deeper as you include him in the trivial things, as
well as the more substantial parts of your life.

Have you ever felt like what you felt didn't matter to anyone
else? Well, it matters to God. King David was far from
perfect, but he was known as a friend of God. Read through
the Psalms and you will find he poured out his heart to God,
no matter what state it was in. Share your heart with God and
deepen your friendship with him today. He cares for you.

Lord, what a liberating idea it is that you are interested
in every detail of my life. I want to know you as a friend,
and I will include you in every part of my life. Reveal your
nearness and love, even as I talk to you throughout my day
and pour out my heart to you.

BEGINNING AND END

"I am the Alpha and the Omega," says the Lord God,
"who is, and who was, and who is to come, the Almighty."
REVELATION 1:8 NIV

God the Almighty is above all. He is outside of the limits
of our understanding. He was at the beginning, creating
everything we see, know, and the things that have yet to be
discovered. He is now, fully with us through his Spirit. He is
still to come, for he never ceases to exist in power and love.

In light of God's vastness, how small do your problems
seem? This is not to say that they are insignificant. You know
that God cares for the things you care about. But he is not
worried about the things that worry you. He is not surprised
by a thing. Find your rest and refuge in his presence today.
May your heart hide in his goodness and may your mind rest
in his peace. He is faithful, powerful, and victorious, and he
always will be.

Everlasting God, I cannot truly comprehend how great you
are, but I trust that you are bigger and better than I can
imagine. Who am I that you would think of me? And yet
you do. I am overwhelmed by your kindness.

HE ALREADY KNOWS

"Your Father knows exactly what you need
even before you ask him!"
MATTHEW 6:8 NLT

Even before you ask him, God already knows your exact
need. May this truth bring comfort and relief to your heart,
as you trust him with your life today. He knows what you
don't even know to ask for. Trust that he will provide what
you need.

We don't have to pray long-winded prayers to be heard
by God. He answers every cry for help, even when it is
just a whisper from the depths of our hearts. It can feel
startling when unexpected crises arise. We can't anticipate
the unknown. But God is faithful, he is wise, and he is
unwavering in power. He does not want us to worry our
lives away, not truly living in the freedom his love offers. He
wants us to rest in the peace of God, expecting that he will
take care of us every step of the way.

Almighty God, you already know what I need today. So,
with simplicity, I pray that you would provide my daily
bread. I choose to walk in your ways. May your kingdom
come, and your will be done on earth, as it is in heaven.

IN THE NAME

Whatever you do in word or deed,
do everything in the name of the Lord Jesus,
giving thanks through him to God the Father.
COLOSSIANS 3:17 NASB

When we adjust our focus each day to offer our work, our sacrifice, and our love to the Lord, we can let go of the demanding voices of the world. If we choose to do the hard things as unto the Lord, the load becomes lighter. Without resentment toward others weighing us down, we can choose to do all things for the audience of our beloved Savior.

When you find yourself struggling to do something with a generous heart today, you can refocus your attention and intention toward doing it for the Lord. He is always worthy, and he won't misunderstand you, take you for granted, or ignore your efforts. Whatever you do in word or deed, do all in the name of the Lord Jesus, giving thanks through Him to God the Father. Notice the shift in your heart and attitude when you do.

Father, thank you for the power of shifting perspective that can turn a chore of drudgery into an opportunity to serve and honor you.

LEAN ON HIS HELP

"Be strong and courageous, and do the work. Don't be afraid or discouraged, for the LORD God, my God, is with you. He won't leave you or abandon you until all the work for the service of the LORD's house is finished."

1 CHRONICLES 28:20 CSB

No matter what the work is that is ahead of us, we can confidently know that God is with us through it all. He will not leave us to work it out on our own, and he will not forsake us in our time of need. With strength and courage, we are called to act.

If you know what you are supposed to do, but you fail to start, progress won't be made. God is not going to do the work that is yours to do, but he will help you along the way. There are some things that only God can do, but there is often work that we can also partner with him to do. We can't neglect our own part. So, let us be strong and of good courage, and act.

Lord, thank you for your help in doing the work you have called me to do. I need you every single day. When I am weak, you are my strength. I take the steps I need to, even when I don't want to, because I know you go with me and offer grace when I need it.

CLARITY OF MIND

God is not a God of confusion but of peace.
1 CORINTHIANS 14:33 ESV

When we are confused, it can be hard to decipher the truth. God never operates in confusion, but in peace. He does not turn us around in circles; he straightens our paths. He brings clarity to our confusion, and peace to our anxiety. There isn't any problem that stumps him. He has solutions for our quandaries.

If you are confused in any area of your life, ask God to give you his peace. The world is a confusing place, but God's presence is not. It is full of light, love, peace, joy, and hope. It is not a place of intimidation, control, or secrecy. God's wisdom is simple, straight-forward, and rooted always in love.

Wise God, speak the simplicity of your truth over my circumstances today. I don't want to be caught up in a web of confusion that you never designed me for. You do not hide so that I can't find you; you are easy to find. Thank you that your wisdom brings the fruit of your Spirit. I trust you.

OBEDIENT DEVOTION

The fear of the LORD is the beginning of knowledge,
but fools despise wisdom and instruction.

PROVERBS 1:7 NKJV

The essence of wisdom, the beginning of all knowledge, is found in the Lord. When we live in obedient devotion to God and his ways, we admit that we don't know best. We are able to be directed by God because our hearts are open to his correction and redirection.

Stubbornness is not a reflection of wisdom, but of foolishness. When we resist admitting when we are wrong, we refuse to leave room for the weakness of our humanity. It is so very important that as children of God we don't close off our hearts from learning. If we already think we know everything there is to know, then every failure will feel catastrophic. Let's open our hearts and be willing to change when we are out of alignment with God's ways, wisdom, and love.

Lord, you are full of wisdom more than anyone else. I don't want to walk in conceit or pride, but in love and humility. I honor you and your nature above all things, and I will redirect and seek forgiveness when I see where I have gone off course. Thank you.

JOYFUL HOPE

Be joyful because you have hope.
Be patient when trouble comes,
and pray at all times.
ROMANS 12:12 NCV

Our great hope is not only an idea. It is an experience of fellowship with the Holy Spirit. Joy overflows from a grateful heart. It is an experience of pure delight. Even if the circumstances of our lives do not seem joyful, we can know the pure joy of the Lord in the midst of them.

As you pray to the Lord today, offer him all that you hope for, all that you need, and every burden you carry. As you hand them over, ask for a divine exchange in return. Do you need hope today? God has it in abundance. Do you need comfort? His presence is full of it. Ask the Holy Spirit to fill you with the goodness of his presence, and be refreshed in the joyful peace, hope, and love he offers.

Holy Spirit, you infuse me with hope in the depths of my soul. Thank you for ministering to me so well every single time. You know exactly what I need today. As I offer you all that I can't control, fill me with the good fruit of your presence. Thank you.

TIMELY REMINDERS

Remind them to never tear down anyone with their words or quarrel, but instead be considerate, humble, and courteous to everyone.

TITUS 3:2 TPT

When we are on the defensive, it is natural to want to return harsh words with cutting ones. But what comes naturally is not always the best way to deal with others. Jesus instructed us to love, not only our friends, but also our enemies. The people we enjoy and those we can't stand. We should not tear others down with our words but look to build them up in encouragement and truth.

Even when others are looking for a fight, we don't have to participate. We can maintain the peace of our own hearts and refuse to be hooked by their advances. Though we cannot control their actions, words, or attitudes, we can certainly do something about our own. Instead of stooping to the level of those who want to demean others, let's do the opposite. Let's remain grounded in love and choose to lift others up in encouragement.

Lord, help me to remain rooted in your love in all my interactions today. When I'm tempted to use my words as weapons, help me to instead choose to use them as a salve. I need you in this.

SUSTAINED BY THE LORD

I lie down and sleep;
I wake again, because the LORD sustains me.
PSALM 3:5 NIV

Before you move on with your day, no matter what has already happened or what is looming over you, take some time to meditate on today's verse. You are here because God has given you another day. Every moment is an opportunity to choose how you want to engage in this gift of life. Who do you want to be? How do you want to be known?

Your life is not a mistake. You are not here by accident. You were created by a thoughtful God who delights in you. There is so much mercy for you today. He has so much to share with you. Will you spend time in his presence, letting him speak his words of life over you? You are here, and he wants you to know him in deeper ways. Here is your invitation; will you take it?

Sustainer, you are the giver of life, and you are my creator. Let me see myself, my life, through your eyes today. Speak to me, show me who you are and what you want for me today. I love you.

LOOSEN YOUR GRIP

"If you try to hang on to your life, you will lose it.
But if you give up your life for my sake, you will save it."
MATTHEW 16:25 NLT

When we hold too tightly to the ideals of our lives, we will inevitably be disappointed. We can plan, dream, and work for what drives us, but there will be hiccups in the road. Let's not spend our energies on things that don't actually matter. Let's align our hearts, lives, and motivations in the nature and kingdom of our God.

Jesus said that we would lose our lives if we try to hang on to them. But if we offer our lives to and for him, we will save them. When we yield leadership of our lives to Jesus, it isn't a copout for responsibility. We still get to choose how we will live, but we also prioritize the nature and ways of Christ. His ways are better than our ways and his thoughts are higher than our thoughts. We can trust him with our lives. Let's loosen our grip and give the reins to Jesus, the author and perfector of our faith.

Jesus Christ, I don't want to hold so tightly to my plans for this life that I refuse to allow your mercy any room to redeem and restore what is broken. I choose to follow you, for you are wonderful, trustworthy, and true. In you, I find abundance of life.

AUTHORITY

All who are being led by the Spirit of God, these are sons of
God. For you have not received a spirit of slavery leading to
fear again, but you have received a spirit of adoption as sons
by which we cry out, "Abba! Father!"

ROMANS 8:14-15 NASB

In Christ, we are adopted as children into the family of God.
He has given us his own name, the authority of Jesus Christ,
as our covering. If we are led by the Spirit of God, we belong
to the family of God. Let no one convince us otherwise.

Look to Jesus, not only in fellowship with the Spirit, but also
in the Scriptures. Get to know what he is like. What did the
prophecies about him foretell? What did his ministry reveal
about the Father? Under Christ, you are free to come to the
Father as boldly as anyone, anywhere, ever has. With the
same friendship David had, you can know the Father, Spirit,
and Son in truth. What a glorious gift this is.

Abba, you are my Father, and I am your child. Lead me in
your love and reveal the power of your authority in my life.
Continue to teach me your ways as I follow you.

PRESS ON

Not that I have already reached the goal or am already perfect, but I make every effort to take hold of it because I also have been taken hold of by Christ Jesus.

PHILIPPIANS 3:12 CSB

You are not at the end of your journey: not in this life, and not with the Lord. No matter how young or old you are, there will be times in your life that you simply need to keep going. Perseverance is needed when the going gets tough. Sometimes it looks like just putting one foot in front of the other. At other times, it is inviting God to help you when you can't move a muscle.

Paul was a scholar of the Scriptures. Not only this, but when Christ encountered him and transformed his life, Paul made it his ambition to know him, to be like him, and to serve him. Even then, Paul was able to say that he hadn't yet obtained the fullness of oneness with Christ. He knew it was a continual journey. He was on his, and you are on yours. Keep pressing on!

Lord Jesus, knowing you completely is the goal of my faith. I don't want to get tripped up or distracted by things that don't matter: not in religion, not in this world, and not in my personal life. I press on to know you more. May that be my prayer every day.

YOU ALREADY KNOW

He has told you, O man, what is good,
and what does the LORD require of you
but to do justice, and to love kindness,
and to walk humbly with your God.

MICAH 6:8 ESV

God's will is not a mystery. It is not some vague thing to grasp or try to figure out. It is simple, and its implications can look different in each of our lives. What does the Lord require of us? As it says in today's verse, it is to do justice, and to love kindness, and to walk humbly with your God. This is no different than the law of love that Jesus described.

God's will for you is not something you have to worry about missing out on. You will do a great many things in your life, but in them all, focus on how you do them. How do you treat others? Is your heart humble and open before the Lord? How does his kindness play out in your actions? These are the things to focus on. Instead of agonizing over what job to take, consider how you can implement these characteristics in whatever you do.

God, thank you for the power of your wisdom and the simplicity of your truth. As I walk with you, I partner with you. I'm so glad that there is freedom and choice as I live my life in you.

WALKING ON WATER

He said, "Come." And when Peter had come down out of the
boat, he walked on the water to go to Jesus.

MATTHEW 14:29 NKJV

All of the disciples were in the boat with Peter when Jesus
told him to come to him on the water. Have you ever
wondered why no one else was invited to join him outside
of the boat? Back up one verse and you will see. When the
disciples first spotted Jesus on the water, they thought he was
a ghost. Jesus sought to calm their fears by reassuring them.
Peter's response was, "Lord, if it is You, command me to
come to You on the water" (Matthew 14:28).

Peter wanted to walk on the water with Jesus, and Jesus
honored his desire. This did not make him any better or worse
than the disciples who remained on the boat. When you have
a desire planted in your heart, reach out to the Lord with it.
He may just invite you into a place of miracles, where as long
as you keep your eyes and faith on him, you will not sink.

Jesus, thank you for knowing my personality and for relating
to me in it. I love that you respond to my bids and requests.
You are so wonderful. May my faith grow stronger in you as
you call me out to new places.

BELIEVE HIM

Jesus paid no attention to what they said.
He told the synagogue leader, "Don't be afraid; just believe."
MARK 5:36 NCV

Sometimes, you just have to ignore the naysayers and listen to what Jesus is telling you. He is trustworthy. Don't be afraid. Believe his Word. He is able to do what is impossible for us. Jairus had just been notified that his daughter had died while they were still on their way to his home. While this was devastating news, this is the context of Jesus' words: "Don't be afraid; just believe."

With God, all things are possible. Dead things come to life. Old dreams are resurrected. Miracles are provided. When Jesus compels you to trust him with your heart, your faith, and your hope, do it. He is able to do far more than anyone else ever could even when the reality is grim and there is nothing you can possibly do on your own. Trust him.

God, I believe you over even the harsh realities I face. You are faithful, and I trust you to guide me with your love. Display your power in my life as I choose to take you at your Word.

TAKEN CARE OF

"People everywhere seem to worry about making a living,
but your heavenly Father knows your every need and will
take care of you."

LUKE 12:30 TPT

Have the pressures of life weighed you down? Perhaps you
feel stuck in cycles of lack, of uncertainty, and of indecision.
Even when you have no idea how you will meet a need, your
heavenly Father knows how. He will take care of you.

Sometimes God will impress on your heart what you need
to do, and sometimes he will miraculously provide. You
don't have to worry, though, not about a thing. He will offer
the solutions for your problems and lead you to a place of
rebuilding when everything has been lost. He is the restorer,
redeemer, and provider. He will not let you waste away. Trust
him, for he is your good Father.

Heavenly Father, I want my trust in your faithfulness to
grow deeper. I know this happens through experience,
relationship, and walking with you. I don't want to worry
about making a living. I choose to trust your goodness and
provision. You are better at piecing things together than I
am. How wonderful you are, and how wonderfully you take
care of your children.

RESTORED BY GOD

"Let their flesh be renewed like a child's;
let them be restored as in the days of their youth
then that person can pray to God and find favor with him,
they will see God's face and shout for joy;
he will restore them to full well-being."

JOB 33:25-26 NIV

Job lost everything. He lost his health, his wealth, and his family. It wasn't because he did anything wrong. Even though he suffered great losses, he did not lose his faith. Even when his friends encouraged him to give up hope, he could not. In the depths of his grief and questions, God did not abandon him. He will not abandon you, either.

There is restoration and renewal coming. He restores what tragedy stole and brings beauty out of the ashes of defeat. If you find yourself in a season of suffering, do not give up hope. Just as surely as the sun rises each morning and sets in the evening, so will the dawn of your God rise upon you. He will bring you relief, and he never leaves you in the valley of the shadow. He works in the details and in the dark, even when you cannot sense it. Redemption is coming, beloved. You will see it. You will know it. You will live it.

Lord, thank you for the power of your restoration. Do it again, Lord, and revive my heart and life in your love.

HEALING IN CONFESSION

Confess your sins to each other and pray for each other so that you may be healed. The earnest prayer of a righteous person has great power and produces wonderful results.

JAMES 5:16 NLT

It can be incredibly healing when we share a confession with those we can trust. What feels like too heavy a weight to carry alone, what grows in the shadows of shame, these things can be lightened and relieved when they are shared with trustworthy people. When someone confesses their shame to you, pray for them. Leave space for them. Speak truth over them. There is healing in this.

If you have a confession to make, don't run to the closest person. Bring it to someone who is reliable, loving, and who will hold you up in prayer. You are not obligated to share the depths of your heart or life with everyone. You can choose who you come to with these vulnerable things. As you pray together, knowing that you are seen, known, and loved, may your heart know the healing balm of true fellowship, and the power of earnest prayers being answered.

Righteous One, I don't want to hide things that need to be brought to the light, but I also don't want to be foolish about who I confess these things to. Give me wisdom to know who is trustworthy and true. Thank you.

GROWING UP IN GOD

Leaving the elementary teaching about the Christ, let us press on to maturity, not laying again a foundation of repentance from dead works and of faith toward God, of instruction about washings and laying on of hands, and the resurrection of the dead and eternal judgment.

HEBREWS 6:1-2 NASB

If we find ourselves drawn to repenting over and over again for things that we feel shame over, then we are caught in childish cycles of insecurity. Our place in God, the power of his forgiveness, and the redemption of his love are enough to remove the power of sin's hold over us.

There are greater stages of faith, of freedom, and of serving the Lord as we partner with his purposes. There is always more to discover in the wisdom of Christ. There is always more for us to learn, greater ways for us to expand in his love, and increased revelation to receive. This happens as we follow the Lord every day. Let's not give into false narratives of having to remain rigid in the religious "righteousness" that others may put upon us.

Father, I don't want my growth in you or your kingdom to become stagnant. I want to keep pressing on to maturity, all while focusing on the things that matter and always will: putting your faith, love, and hope into practice.

REAP WHAT YOU SOW

Let us not get tired of doing good,
for we will reap at the proper time if we don't give up.
GALATIANS 6:9 CSB

Now is always the time to do what is right. Today is the only day we have guaranteed us. How will we choose to live it? In verse 7 of the same chapter in Galatians, Paul says, "Do not be deceived; God is not mocked, for you reap whatever you sow." If you sow bitterness and division, you will reap it. If you sow kindness and mercy, you will reap that.

Focus on doing the right thing today, no matter how difficult it may feel at the time. Don't give up on the ways of God, for you will reap a reward every time you choose them. Though you may have to wait for the fruit, it will come. Don't neglect the seeds you sow today, for they will produce a crop in the coming season.

Righteous One, thank you for the power of your nature that draws us in with mercy-kindness over and over again. I want to be like you. Help me to choose rightly today in my actions and interactions. I want to sow seeds for your kingdom.

CHRIST OUR HEAD

Speaking the truth in love, we are to grow up in every way
into him who is the head, into Christ, from whom the whole
body, joined and held together by every joint with which it
is equipped, when each part is working properly, makes the
body grow so that it builds itself up in love.

EPHESIANS 4:15-16 ESV

If we are aligned in the nature of Christ, we will build each
other up in love. If our connection to each other is rooted in
who Christ is and what he wants for each of us, then we will
not neglect to do our part while also caring for one another.

Though you may look at the gifts of another child of God
and feel small in comparison, do not overlook the beauty,
dignity, and power of your role in the family of God. We
cannot all be eyes or hands. Let's continue to grow up in
every way into Christ, who is our head. Let's embrace the gift
of our role and use it to build others up in love. This is the
way of Christ and his kingdom.

Christ, I am grateful for who I am in you. Help me to serve
others in love and do my part well. May I mature in your
truth and leave room for the gifts and strengths of others.

UNSHAKEABLE TRUST

The king was overjoyed and gave orders to take Daniel out of
the den. When Daniel was brought up from the den, he was
found to be unharmed, for he trusted in his God.

DANIEL 6:23 CSB

The story of Daniel in the lion's den is a miraculous one. God
shut the mouths of the lions and kept Daniel from harm.
Though we cannot predict what dangers we may go through
in life, we can trust God through them all.

It all comes back to our connection to the Lord. We each
have a unique relationship to him. His love, his grace, his
power, and his peace are always available. We don't have to
search the world for his goodness. It is found with us, even
when we are in a lion's den.

My God, I love that you are powerful beyond measure,
overwhelming in kindness toward you children, and that
you are accessible to me here and now. May the trust of
my heart build as you continue to reveal yourself to me. I
belong to you.

CHOOSING FORGIVENESS

Bear with each other, and forgive each other.
If someone does wrong to you,
forgive that person because the Lord forgave you.
COLOSSIANS 3:13 NCV

It is not always easy to choose to forgive those around us.
Some hurts cut deeper than others. Even so, God is with
us in the process. He gives us grace, and he honors our
willingness. Forgiveness can take time, but it also takes
intention. You can forgive someone and not resume the same
closeness of relationship you once had. You can bear with
them, and still choose how you interact with them.

The Lord is quick to forgive. He is able to do it perfectly.
Don't despair if you find it difficult. He does not shame you
for your weakness. He is your Father and your help. He
offers his compassion and mercy to mend your wounds and
help you to move on. As you choose forgiveness, even if you
must do it over and over again, know that God sees your
movement and he honors it.

Merciful Father, thank you for your grace. I don't want to
become bitter with unforgiveness. Help me to truly forgive
those who hurt me and to let go and trust you. May love
cover a multitude of sins, just as it has covered mine.

FOUND IN HIM

It is through him that we live and function and have our
identity; just as your own poets have said, "Our lineage
comes from him."

ACTS 17:28 TPT

The New Living Translation starts today's verse this way:
"For in him we live and move and exist." In Christ we live,
move, and have our being. He is our identity, and that is
a powerful statement. Christ, our Redeemer and Victor
is the one in whom we find ourselves fully alive and fully
identified.

God is in art, in movement, and in poetry. He is in creative
expressions, as well as the sciences. Connect to God spirit
to Spirit today through a creative outlet. Whether you dance
before him, paint a picture in his presence, or simply breathe
in and out with acute awareness of his nearness, turn your
attention to the one who calls you his own. Let your heart
respond in active ways today. You are found in him, and he
is your Father.

Good Father, in you I live and function and have my very
identity. I am your child, and you are my good Father.
Be honored through my surrendered acts of creative
connection today.

OCTOBER

Be anxious for nothing, but
in everything by prayer and
supplication, with thanksgiving,
let your requests be made known
to God; and the peace of God,
which surpasses all understanding,
will guard your hearts and minds
through Christ Jesus.

PHILIPPIANS 4:6-7 NKJV

HELP ME BELIEVE

Immediately the boy's father exclaimed, "I do believe; help me overcome my unbelief!"

MARK 9:24 NIV

When Jesus said, "Everything is possible for one who believes," the immediate response of the father whose son was tormented was "I do believe; help me overcome my unbelief!" The father recognized in himself the desire to believe while also admitting that he wasn't fully there.

We don't have to hide our lack of faith before Jesus. He knows our hearts, after all. If we have even a seed of faith, it can grow to move mountains. This is what Jesus revealed through the parable of the mustard seed. May we not discount the smallness of our faith when God can partner with it to make it grow. He is a help to us in all things, even in overcoming our unbelief.

Miracle Worker, I know that everything is possible for you and for those who believe. Increase my faith as I continue to walk in your ways. I believe that you can do the impossible; help my unbelief!

ASKED AND GRANTED

The LORD grants wisdom!
From his mouth come knowledge and understanding.
PROVERBS 2:6 NLT

When we seek after understanding, we find it in the Lord. He offers wisdom to all who earnestly search for it. As long as we are open and looking for insight, God will grant it to us. He does not trick us. As we come to the Lord in prayer, he answers us with his goodness.

Jesus said, "You parents, if your children ask for a loaf of bread, do you give them a stone instead? So, if you… know how to give good gifts to your children, how much more will your heavenly Father give good gifts to those who ask him" (Matthew 7:9, 11). You don't have to wonder whether God will give you the clarity you need when you look to him. He is infinitely wise, better than even the best of men, and will not delay. Trust him to answer you, for he will.

Lord, as I come to you for answers, direction, and wisdom, I trust you to give it to me. I will rest in the peace of your presence as I wait on your reply. Thank you.

KINGDOM ATTRIBUTES

The kingdom of God is not eating and drinking, but
righteousness and peace and joy in the Holy Spirit.
ROMANS 14:17 NASB

The kingdom of God is not made up of rules and
regulations. It is not about what you eat, how you dress, or
any outer expression. It is full of the fruit of God's Spirit.
Righteousness, peace, and joy can all be found in a myriad of
ways in the earth and in the kingdom of God.

The Holy Spirit's fruit is always as described in Galatians
5, every expression of the expansive nature of God. It is
love, joy, peace, patience, kindness, goodness, faithfulness,
gentleness, and self-control. Instead of getting caught up on
the particulars that don't matter, let's focus more on the heart
behind them. Righteousness, peace, and joy are found in the
kingdom of God, and as we join our choices to the ways of
God, we will see this fruit sprout up in our lives.

Great God, I don't want to be distracted by the form and
function of faith. I want to live from a place of rooted and
grounded love as I follow your ways. May the fruit of your
kingdom be apparent in my life as I partner with your
purposes.

NOURISHING GRACE

I commit you to God and to the word of his grace, which is able to build you up and to give you an inheritance among all who are sanctified.

ACTS 20:32 CSB

The message of God's grace is nourishing and life-giving. It builds us up into the love of Christ. We grow in grace, even as we receive more of the generosity of God's mercy toward us. We cannot earn grace or lose it. We cannot limit it or its strength.

Feast on the grace of God today as you spend time in his presence. Ask the Lord for greater revelations of his goodness that will build your courage, your hope, and your heart in him. If you are in Christ, you are fully washed in the mercy of his heart. You are completely covered in his grace. It never runs out, it fills every crack, and it continues to powerfully strengthen us each and every day.

Generous Father, thank you for the message of your grace and the power of it in my life. I believe that it is all I need today. Strengthen me in the areas I am weak and continue to build me up in the truth of who you are. Thank you.

POWER OF SCRIPTURE

All Scripture is breathed out by God and profitable for
teaching, for reproof, for correction, and for training in
righteousness, that the man of God may be complete,
equipped for every good work.

2 TIMOTHY 3:16-17 ESV

The power of God's Word is in its intention and inspiration.
Though we see human frailty clearly displayed in Scripture,
we also see the unrelenting mercy of God thread throughout
it. There is wisdom in the teachings of Scripture and helpful
corrections for our missteps. There is goodness in its practice.

The Holy Spirit still breathes on our hearts and minds as
we read the Word today. There is revelation in his presence
to instruct us in deeper understanding of the ways of God.
The kingdom of God is revealed through the power of Jesus'
ministry. There is more than enough to help us when we
need it. Don't neglect the foundation of Scripture as a way to
know God and to become more like him.

Righteous One, thank you for revealing your character
through Scripture, even when it so starkly lies in contrast to
the habits of humankind. Thank you that you are merciful,
faithful, and true. You are just, kind, and unrelenting in love.
Teach me more about you today as I delve into your Word.

ROOM FOR WEAKNESS

I take pleasure in infirmities, in reproaches, in needs,
in persecutions, in distresses, for Christ's sake.
For when I am weak, then I am strong.

2 CORINTHIANS 12:10 NKJV

Though it may seem like foolishness to take pleasure in the
hardest areas of life, when we learn to lean on the grace
of God in every circumstance, his strength flows into our
weakness. Though we cannot get through on our own, he
carries us through with the power of his presence.

We are not taught to embrace our weakness, though it is
a strength if we learn to do it. We are not perfect, and we
cannot expect ourselves to be. When we leave room for
weakness, error, and mistakes, we make space for God's
grace to do in and for us what we cannot on our own. With
humble hearts, we learn the power of God in the midst of
pain, suffering, and distress. Christ is very real and very
present with us through his Spirit. It is a gift to lean into his
help and to have the opportunity to do so.

Gracious God, thank you for the empowering grace of your
presence that meets me in my weakness. I want to learn, as
Paul did, to delight in suffering, not because it is fun, but
because you are with me in it. Teach me, refine me, and
increase my understanding of your love as you carry me
through hardship.

HIS KINDNESS

I will tell about the LORD's kindness
and praise him for everything he has done.
He has shown great mercy to us
and has been very kind to us.

ISAIAH 63:7 NCV

When you think about God's mercy and kindness, how have
you seen it displayed in your own life? For every relief of a
need, for everything restored that was once lost, is a story
to tell. Take some time to think about the specific kindness
of God in your personal walk with him. Don't worry if it
doesn't automatically come to mind. Ask the Holy Spirit to
remind you of God's hand in your life.

As you recall what God's kindness and mercy have meant
to you, allow your heart to respond as it will. Spend time
in the presence of God, thanking him and worshiping him.
This can take as little or as long as you like. When you go
about your day, consider who you can share a testimony
of his goodness with. Don't hesitate to share your heartfelt
experience with someone today. It may encourage their own
hearts to remember, or even to look to God for his kindness
in their lives right now.

Kind God, thank you for your goodness toward me. I
worship you.

FROM WORRY TO FAITH

"Don't worry or surrender to your fear.
For you've believed in God,
now trust and believe in me also."

JOHN 14:1 TPT

Jesus' invitation to you today is to lay down your fear and worry. Don't give into the anxieties that flood your heart and mind. Instead, offer them to him. As you do, believe that he will take care of you, for he promises to do so.

What are the worries and fears that threaten your peace? What are the things you have not been able to shake off? Ignoring them won't fix the weight of their existence. However, offering them to Christ in exchange for his perfect peace may be just what you need. Even when fear rises up, you don't have to drown in it. Pray out your fears, receive the grace of God to strengthen your heart in hope, and choose to take Christ at his word. He won't let you down.

Faithful One, I choose to give you every worry and anxiety on my heart and in my mind today. I won't stop until they're all laid out before you. I choose to believe that you will take care of them, no matter if I can't see how. I trust you.

DAILY SURRENDER

He said to them all: "Whoever wants to be my disciple must deny themselves and take up their cross daily and follow me."

LUKE 9:23 NIV

What does it mean to follow Jesus? Is it just that we talk about him every once in a while, go to church once a week, and call ourselves Christians? Following Jesus isn't about an ideology, and it's not exclusive to the religious. Jesus said, "Whoever wants to be my disciple must deny themselves and take up their cross daily and follow me."

Daily surrender to the Lord and his leadership is at the heart of our walk with the Lord. If we want to truly follow Jesus, it requires a denial of self in some regard. It means that we put his ways above our own, take up the challenges in front of us, and follow him, no matter the cost. Let's not forget that Christ is kind, wise, and powerful. He will never lead us down a path he has not already tread.

Lord, I surrender to your will and ways today. I won't try to excuse my lack of trust in you. I choose to follow you, and I know that requires denial of opposing values. I take what is mine and bring it to you, and I trust you to lead me in truth.

IDENTIFIABLE FRUIT

"Just as you can identify a tree by its fruit,
so you can identify people by their actions."
MATTHEW 7:20 NLT

When we see chaos surrounding and following a person, no matter where they go, we can be sure the fruit of their lives is showing. When a person is kind, honorable, and hardworking, the fruit of their lives is also undeniable. We must align our values with our actions. Out of the priorities of our hearts, we will live.

A bad tree will only bear rotten fruit (Matthew 7:18). A good tree will produce good fruit. One of the best ways to recognize the character of a person is what they do after they mess up or have been called out. If they are proud, deflecting responsibility, this is not the fruit of a humble heart. If they are willing to admit their mistakes and take accountability for them, they reveal that they prioritize humility, personal responsibility, and the chance to learn and grow. Let's be wise in our estimations of others, while also remaining humble in our own hearts.

Wise God, thank you for the discernment of your truth at work in people's lives including mine. I want to live a good life, with your kingdom values as my own. I humble myself before you and commit to admitting when I'm wrong with others.

FIRST THING

In the morning, LORD, you will hear my voice;
in the morning I will present my prayer to you
and be on the watch.

PSALM 5:3 NASB

When you woke up this morning, what was the first thing you did? What were the first words you spoke and to whom did you speak them? Don't feel guilty if it was something other than praying to God. He does not count your habits against you. He loves any time you come to him.

Consider the benefits of coming to the Lord first thing in the morning. Try, as soon as you are consciously awake, to turn your attention to the Lord in some way. Whether it's a "good morning, Lord" or a "help me get up and get ready on time," reach out to him the next few days as soon as you wake up and see how it sets the tone for your day. Perhaps it will be a new practice that brings peace and joy.

Ever-Present One, I'm so grateful for your nearness every moment of every day. As I train my heart and mind to connect with you first thing in the morning, speak to me while I am still waking up and refresh me with your words of life. Thank you.

LEARNING OPPORTUNITIES

It was good for me to be afflicted
so that I could learn your statutes.
PSALM 119:71 CSB

When we fail, do we wallow in self-recrimination or pity,
or do we take the opportunity to learn from our mistakes?
Every failure is a chance to grow in wisdom. We may not
be able to go back in time and change what has already
happened, but we can choose how we act from here on out.

As children, we are accustomed to learning, both in big ways
and little ways. As we mature, we sometimes forget that
we still don't know it all. We will never be perfect, either,
so we can't always get it right. Failure is certain. Dejection,
however, isn't. May we shift our thinking and expectations
around each humbling of our hearts and use each as an
opportunity to learn what God says about it. He is so wise,
and he always has a solution even in our failures.

Great God, learning to let go of perfectionism and pride
is one of the hardest parts about growing into maturity.
However, the weight of them are not what we were meant
for. Use each humbling of my heart and pride to teach me
the beauty of your ways.

NO LINGERING ACCUSATIONS

There is therefore now no condemnation
for those who are in Christ Jesus.
ROMANS 8:1 ESV

In order to get the full power of today's verse, we can
look at the preceding statement. Why is there no more
condemnation for those who are in Christ? Even though
we want to obey God's law, our nature is prone to sin.
This is why we mess up over and over again. However, the
answer is in Jesus Christ our Lord. He is our salvation, our
redemption, and our liberation.

God did what we could never do; he provided the sacrifice
that the law required. He sent his Son in our place, for once
and for all people. This is why, even when accusing voices
of shame try to convince us of our complete and utter guilt,
in Christ we experience relief and freedom. "Who shall
bring any charge against God's elect? It is God who justifies"
(Romans 8:33). If God has justified us, we are free from
condemnation, for now and for always.

Redeemer, thank you for the power of your sacrifice over
sin, death, and every fear and shame. You are better than life
itself, and you are my soul's liberation. I am free here and
now, completely covered in your mercy.

GREATER THAN ANY ARMY

"This is the word of the LORD to Zerubbabel:
'Not by might nor by power, but by my Spirit,'
says the LORD of hosts."

ZECHARIAH 4:6 NKJV

Though great feats of strength may impress us, they are nothing in comparison to the power of God. Nothing is impossible for him. By the Spirit of God, mountains are moved, the sick are healed, and the dead raised. The resurrection power of Christ's life is greater than any show of force in this world.

Has fear got a hold of your heart? When you look at the state of the world, are you discouraged? Look to the one who created the heavens and the earth. Align your heart in the great power of God's love today. He is just as able to move in miraculous moves of mercy today as he was in Biblical times. He has not stopped moving. Trust him and look for the move of his Spirit.

Spirit of God, move in the world to bring peace, clarity, and justice. Move also in my life in mercy. I need you. We all need you.

DWELLING PLACE

Don't you know that you are God's temple
and that God's Spirit lives in you?
1 CORINTHIANS 3:16 NCV

You don't have to wait to find God in a sacred place or in a
religious setting. You are God's temple. The Spirit of God
makes his home in you. Wherever you are, if you are in
Christ, then the sacred place of meeting is inside of you.

Take a moment right now to close your eyes, turning your
attention to your heart. In the depths of you is where God
dwells. If you are Christ's, then you are home in him, and
he is at home in you. You don't lack anything today, for you
have the fullness of God's Spirit within you. Where deep calls
to deep in your soul, there is the holy of holies. There is the
place of meeting. If God has sanctified you, then you are holy.
Meditate on that as you commune with him, spirit to Spirit.

Lord God, thank you that I don't have to go anywhere to
meet with you. Right here, right in this place I inhabit, you
are with me. You are in me. Love me to life from the inside
out, Worthy One.

MORE THAN A THEORY

Beloved children, our love can't be an abstract theory we only talk about, but a way of life demonstrated through our loving deeds.

1 JOHN 3:18 TPT

If the love of God is only something we talk about, we miss out on its true power. The love of God is a force. It is found in active pursuit. It is in laid-down-service to one another. If we talk about how much we love God and yet don't have any loving deeds to point to, then our words are empty. Our faith is empty.

True love acts. The love of God moved heaven and earth, sending Christ to earth as the image of the Father, laying down his life so that we might be completely free to know him. He is our salvation, and we cannot extricate his love from anything that he ever did, still does, or is yet to do. The mercy of God in action is all that matters. We must go past theories and endless talk and put our faith into practice. We must love by demonstrating it through our choices. No good deed is overlooked, but those who only talk and never follow-through cannot be trusted.

Lord, I'm so grateful that your love is an active force, not just a theory or idea. I choose to follow you by being practical in kindness, mercy, and love. I follow your example.

COVENANT OF PEACE

"Though the mountains be shaken
and the hills be removed,
yet my unfailing love for you will not be shaken
nor my covenant of peace be removed,"
says the LORD, who has compassion on you.

ISAIAH 54:10 NIV

Even when the chaos of the world heightens, the covenant of God's peace is unshakeable. It remains steadfast and true. What God promises, he does. He is faithful in all ways, in all times, and to all who trust in him. The unfailing love of God is not lacking; in fact, it is ever-moving in overwhelming measure. When we see wickedness rising, let's remember that God's love overpowers it, even still.

God's presence brings peace to our inner worlds, even when our outer worlds are turned upside-down. Meditate on God's unfailing love, the compassion he has that will never be removed. He is able to do far more than you can imagine, and what he does is good. May you know the confidence of his faithfulness toward you, for he never fails.

Powerful One, thank you for the reminder that no matter what is going on in my life or in the world, you are bigger still. You are still full of unfailing love, resurrection power, and incomparable wisdom. You will never fail, and I choose to trust you.

PROMISE OF PRESENCE

"I will be with you as I was with Moses.
I will not fail you or abandon you.
Be strong and courageous."

JOSHUA 1:5-6 NLT

Have you ever felt as if God was too far away? Perhaps you missed out on what he once had for you? It is never too late to follow him. It's never past time to draw near. He is already close. When you turn to him, he rushes to meet you.

He promises to be with you as he was with Moses. Even Moses did not have the Spirit of God dwelling within him. He is known as a father of the faith, and we get the same access that he had. This is almost too much to comprehend, too good to be true. Be strong and courageous, not because you have to not show any weakness, but because God is with you even in your weakness. He promises his presence, even to the end of the age. You don't have to miss out on a moment of fellowship, for he is near.

My God, thank you for seeing me, knowing me, and for being with me. I am yours. Even when I am afraid, I will trust in you. I will press on in courage and lean on your grace-strength when I am weak. Be near, Lord, and speak to me. Lead me. I am going with you.

MEASURES OF MERCY

He saved us, not on the basis of deeds which we did in righteousness, but in accordance with his mercy, by the washing of regeneration and renewing by the Holy Spirit.

TITUS 3:5 NASB

It is important to remember your own agency in this life. You get to choose how you will grow, what steps you will take, and how you treat people. Your choices matter. Still, it is even more important to recognize that none of these choices adds to or takes away from your salvation. You are saved by mercy alone. It is all the work of Christ. You can't convince him to save you any more, for he has already done it. Every choice, then, reflects how you want to live. How you want to be known. How you want to interact with others.

The measures of God's mercy are endless. Your victories don't make Christ's mercy any more powerful, just as your failures cannot diminish it one bit. May you find freedom in this truth. Christ's mercy is his alone, and his alone to offer. He offers it freely. He is your salvation.

Christ, thank you for the power of your sacrifice and for the renewal of your Spirit in my life. You take the pressure off of following you perfectly, and instead give me the freedom to follow you well. Thank you.

PERFECT LOVE

There is no fear in love;
instead, perfect love drives out fear,
because fear involves punishment.
So the one who fears is not complete in love.

1 JOHN 4:18 CSB

The work of God's perfect love is to drive out fear, to liberate us from shame, and to free us to walk in the light of his presence. There is no fear in love. As God removes fear from our hearts, we no longer worry about how we could mess up. Even when we fail, God's love is strong enough to restore us. Letting fear restrict our expectations and our actions does not move us closer to God's love, but further from it. We cannot destroy our standing with God when he has already covered us completely in the mercy of Christ.

When you feel fear pushing or pulling you into restrictive thinking, action, or relating, ask the Lord to flood you with his perfect love once more. His love makes space, brings clarity, and calms the nervous system. His presence brings peace.

Loving Lord, there is so much fear at work in the world. I don't want to be motivated by fear but by your perfect love. I make room for you.

GIFTS OF GRACE

As each has received a gift, use it to serve one another,
as good stewards of God's varied grace.
1 PETER 4:10 ESV

Our talents, gifts, and strengths are not only for our own
benefit. We were created for community, and each of us has
a role to play in it. What we are gifted at, we can use to serve
one another in love. May we resist the pull of society that seeks
to monetize every passion and instead know when to offer
specific gifts and services as a generous offering to others.

How can you use your natural strengths, interests, or talents
to serve people in your community? It doesn't have to be an
all-or-nothing venture. Recognize what you have to give,
what you are willing to offer, and implement actionable
levels of service. Even if you start small, that small beginning
is a beautiful representation of God's kingdom. We are
stronger when we are connected to each other. Look for ways
to uplift those who need it in your community. You just may
inspire others to do the same.

Gracious God, thank you for the example of service you
showed us through Christ. I don't want to forget the
importance of connectedness and community. Show me
ways I can use my gifts to serve those around me.

CHEERFUL CHOICES

Let each one give as he purposes in his heart,
not grudgingly or of necessity;
for God loves a cheerful giver.
2 CORINTHIANS 9:7 NKJV

God loves a cheerful giver. We've probably all heard this many times in our church days. He does. He loves a cheerful giver. Yet, there is absolutely no tinge of guilt or manipulation in this truth. Others may have tried to use this verse to create a response in those who they were speaking to, yet God has no need to manipulate us. It is not how he works.

Let each one give as he purposes in his heart. Whatever you choose to give, if there is no grudge against it or hesitation in your heart, then you can give it freely. Giving reflects our generous Father, it is true. The more we practice stretching our own generosity, the easier it becomes. Still, it is important that we give what we choose to, not what anyone else pressures us into. Let us give out of a cheerful heart, letting go of the need to micromanage it at all (there should be no strings attached to a gift). As we do, we honor God and clear our own consciences.

Generous One, thank you for your abundant and magnanimous gifts to us. I want to be more like you in my giving. I will not give grudgingly or because I feel pressured to, but only out of what I choose to.

LEAVE SOME ROOM

Always be humble and gentle.
Be patient with each other,
making allowance for each other's faults
because of your love.

EPHESIANS 4:2 NLT

Having a humble and gentle heart not only serves us well; it serves those around us, as well. We must remember that we are all human and prone to error. When we leave room for each other's faults, there is space for grace. We know what it is to fail others' expectations and what it is to have our own unmet. Do we hope that those around us are able to make allowance for our faults? If we hope to be treated with patience, we must also pursue that same patience in our hearts toward others.

When we keep love alive in our hearts, we are able to adjust and readjust our expectations. With patience as a priority, we can walk through our faults and flaws together. Not every fault needs to be confronted, though some will. Even then, with humble hearts, gentle approaches, and genuine love, we can bridge the gap.

Faithful One, you are so patient and gentle with me. Why would I refuse to be with others? Thank you for the grace of your Spirit that helps me.

OPPORTUNITIES TO BLESS

Take advantage of every opportunity to be a blessing to others, especially to our brothers and sisters in the family of faith!

GALATIANS 6:10 TPT

When we cultivate generosity in our hearts and lives, we begin to look for opportunities to bless others instead of just waiting for them to appear. Every chance to bless someone is an opportunity for our own joy.

Romans 12:10 says, "Be devoted to tenderly loving your fellow believers as members of one family. Try to outdo yourselves in respect and honor of one another." What would it look like for you to try to outdo what you have done before in offering respect and honor to others? What would it look like to be devoted to tenderly loving your fellow believers? Look for ways to bless others, and you will find them. There is so much joy for you as you partner with God in this way.

Marvelous One, I truly want to be part of a body of believers that tries to outdo each other in offering practical kindness, respect, and honor. I know that this can start with me. I choose to look for ways to bless others. I know there is so much satisfaction and blessing for me as I partner with you in this way.

POWERFUL PRUDENCE

The tongue is a small part of the body, but it makes great boasts. Consider what a great forest is set on fire by a small spark.

JAMES 3:5 NIV

Just one small comment can set off a fiery argument. When we practice prudence with our words, reining in our tongues when we need to, we practice wisdom. There is power in the words we speak. Let's not treat them as meaningless, then, for they have the ability to either build up or tear down the hearer.

As you engage in conversation today, whether face to face or through technology, be sure to pick your words wisely. Though you don't have to be perfect, just practice prudence. Think before you send the email. Consider the comment before you leave it. Proverbs 17:28 says, "Even fools are thought wise if they keep silent, and discerning if they hold their tongues."

Wise Father, help me to think through what I say. I don't want to be foolish, causing harm with thoughtless words. May I be wise and thoughtful, just as you are at all times. I know it's a worthwhile pursuit.

SPIRIT OF TRUTH

"When the Spirit of truth comes, he will guide you into all truth. He will not speak on his own but will tell you what he has heard."

JOHN 16:13 NLT

The Spirit of God is the Spirit of truth. There is no other. The Holy Spirit guides us into the ways of God, the truth of his nature, and the incomparable goodness of his kingdom. He reveals the God to each of us, making our understanding much deeper than the surface of intellect.

If we are in Christ, we are no longer waiting for the Spirit of truth to come. The Holy Spirit was already poured out. We have the holy Helper with us: the Spirit of God himself to lead us into truth. And we have not yet learned all there is to know. There is more truth to discover, more aspects of God's character, and still the fruit is always the same. May we refrain from being satisfied with stale bread when the Spirit offers us fresh manna to satisfy our hearts and minds in Christ each and every day. There is a fresh portion even now.

Spirit, thank you for continually guiding me into truth. I am not afraid of wandering, for I am following your leadership. May the eyes of my heart be enlightened even more as I taste the fresh manna of God's Word that you offer today.

MORE THAN IDEOLOGY

The kingdom of God is not in words,
but in power.

1 CORINTHIANS 4:20 NASB

The power of God is not in what he says he will do, but in what he actually does. This is true in our own lives. If we are able to talk a good game but fail to actually follow through, then our words are meaningless. However, if we do what we say, doing the work of it, then we back up our words with the weight of our action.

God's kingdom is not an ideology. It is an actual place with an actual reigning King. We may not yet see it, but we catch glimpses of it in the earth as God releases his mercy and faithfully follows through on his Word. Do we truly believe in the power of God's kingdom, or have we simply grown accustomed to the idea of it?

King Jesus, I know that your promises are not empty.
You are working in my life and in the world in marvelous acts of mercy, and you aren't finished yet. Peel back my understanding even more today, as you reveal how you are working here and now.

MULTIPLIED EFFORTS

The one who provides seed for the sower and bread for food will also provide and multiply your seed and increase the harvest of your righteousness.

2 CORINTHIANS 9:10 CSB

God does not only supply seed to the sower, but he multiplies our efforts with the gracious generosity of his power. All that you need comes from him, and he multiplies its effect as you put it to work. This is extraordinarily good news.

Verse 11 of this same chapter continues, "You will be enriched in every way for your great generosity, which will produce thanksgiving to God through us." God can use you to provide for others' needs, just as surely as he uses others to provide for yours. Sometimes the provision is completely supernatural, but often it happens through the generosity of our choices. May we delight in our provider, even as we look for ways to help cover the needs of others. Even these things he multiplies.

Generous Father, thank you for your power that multiplies the provision we both give and receive. You are wonderful.

PERFECT PORTION

"The LORD is my portion," says my soul,
"therefore I will hope in him."
LAMENTATIONS 3:24 ESV

God is a perfect portion for every need at every time. He has more than enough grace for our lack. He has overwhelming mercy for our missteps. He has abundant peace for our fear. He has it all. Whatever needs we experience today, God is an abundantly generous provider.

As we receive from the overflow of God's great nature, there is grace for the cracks in our lives. Though our parents aren't perfect, God is the perfect parent. Though our friends may disappoint us, God never will. Though even the most well-intentioned of people will misunderstand us, God always knows our hearts completely. He is a perfect portion, no matter the lack. We can let the pressure off of others, knowing we can find fullness in him.

Perfect Lord, you are always more than enough for every need I have. I trust that you won't let me down, and you won't disregard me. My heart overflows with gratitude for all that you are. I love you.

HOPEFUL RETURNS

"Return to the stronghold,
you prisoners of hope.
Even today I declare
that I will restore double to you."
ZECHARIAH 9:12 NKJV

God is a master restorer. He not only fixes what was broken, but he multiplies what was lost and returns it to us. He is so very good. If there is any hope in our hearts, any reason to look to the Lord with expectation, it is because he is faithful.

If there is an area of your life that has been barren, with a longing in your heart to return, know that the Lord will offer you more than you once had as he restores you. He is a God of redemption and restoration. No one is too far-gone, and no loss is too devastating that his resurrection power cannot bring new life out of it. Trust him with your heart and with your desires. Put your hope in him, for he will not let you down.

Faithful One, thank you for knowing when and how to restore what you promise to. I trust you with my heart and my life. I know that you are good, and all my hope is in you.

SENSE OF BELONGING

He gave himself for us so he might pay the price to free us from all evil and to make us pure people who belong only to him—people who are always wanting to do good deeds.

TITUS 2:14 NCV

Jesus gave himself for us. That is no small statement. He gave himself for us so that we could freely and wholly belong to him. He paid the price no one else could pay. He did it so that we could know him and belong to him, without any doubt or barrier between us.

You belong in the kingdom of Christ. There is a place specifically for you. No one can take it. No one can replace you. You are his, and he loves you more than you can imagine. If you struggle to find your place in this world, know that you need not struggle to find yourself in him. He does not mistake your intentions or misunderstand you. He sees you, he loves you, and he accepts you.

Savior, I cannot begin to describe my gratitude for all that you did on the cross. Thank you for saving me. I am yours, and I find myself at home in you.

NOVEMBER

Set your minds on things that are above, not on things that are on earth. For you have died, and your life is hidden with Christ in God.

Colossians 3:2-3 esv

EVERY GENERATION

Yahweh is always good and ready to receive you. He's so loving that it will amaze you— so kind that it will astound you! And he is famous for his faithfulness toward all. Everyone knows our God can be trusted, for he keeps his promises to every generation!

PSALM 100:5 TPT

The Lord is good and ready to receive you today. His love is so tender that it will amaze you. He is so kind that it will blow you away. His faithfulness is not reserved for an elite few. He is known for his faithfulness toward all. He is trustworthy and true throughout the ages and to every generation.

Let this be a jumping off point to your own personal experience with God today. He is closer than you realize, and more powerful than you know. You don't have to hesitate for fear of his reception. He has arms wide open, ready to receive you just as you are. Run into the arms of your Lord and be loved to life in his presence.

Wonderful Lord, you are faithful to every promise, including to this generation I am living in. Thank you for the power of your love that spans every distance. Refresh me in your kindness and the truth of your love again today.

REVERENT HEARTS

Since we are receiving a kingdom that cannot be shaken,
let us be thankful, and so worship God acceptably with
reverence and awe.

HEBREWS 12:28 NIV

Only the unshakeable remains in the kingdom of God. In
the refinement of life, we may lose many things, but we will
never lose fellowship with God or anything he offers from
his generous heart. With this truth at the forefront of our
thoughts, we can offer God the reverence and awe he is so
very worthy of.

Take some time in your day to remember that only what is
temporary can be shaken. The systems of this world may
topple, and the earth itself may move, but the steadfast
mercy of God will not be deterred. Thank God for the
unwavering aspects of his nature that stand firm, not only
his kingdom, but in your life. Every time you feel awe wash
over your heart, honor the power of it and offer it to the
Lord with reverence.

Worthy God, you are unbreakable and unshakeable. Your
power is not threatened by any person or nation. You are
greater than the systems of this world, and your kingdom
will never falter. Thank you that I belong to you and your
immovable kingdom of grace.

PATIENT ENDURANCE

Do not throw away this confident trust in the Lord.
Remember the great reward it brings you! Patient endurance
is what you need now, so that you will continue to do God's
will. Then you will receive all that he has promised.

HEBREWS 10:35-36 NLT

When hard times linger on longer than we expected, it can
be tempting to give up what once felt so important to us. If
God has been a lifeline to you, don't give up hope in him.
He has not forgotten what he promised, and he never leaves
you. Even when you can't sense what he is doing, he is still
working in the details of your life.

Patient endurance is a fruit of the Spirit, and it is also an
important part of our faith. Why is this? Because without it,
at the first sign of trouble, we would walk away. God never
promised us an easy life. Jesus did not say that we would
escape suffering in this life, in fact he promised the opposite.
Life is full of peaks and valleys, and none is permanent.
Trust the Lord, keep following him, and you will see that he
is as faithful as you dared to hope he would be.

Faithful One, I need the grace of your presence to help me.
Help me to endure through seasons of pain with patience,
unwavering in hope and holding on to you through it all.

EYES THAT SEE

Our struggle is not against flesh and blood, but against the rulers, against the powers, against the world forces of this darkness, against the spiritual forces of wickedness in the heavenly places.

EPHESIANS 6:12 NASB

Jesus said in Matthew 13:16, "Blessed are your eyes, because they see; and your ears, because they hear." When we follow the Lord, looking to him for leadership, wisdom, and strength, we will not miss his redirections when they come. We must realize when we struggle with those around us, it is not a fight against who they are. There are forces at work that we cannot see. Let's not lose sight of this and allow our hearts to grow cold against one another.

Eyes that see and ears that hear, that is what Christ offers us. We have full fellowship with his Spirit that offers us a different perspective from the limited one we have. Though we see from a low-level, God is higher than all of it and still doesn't miss a detail. Let's join God and look from his lens. As we put on love and heed the wisdom of God, our eyes will be opened to the humanity of those we struggle with.

Perfect One, I don't want to hate those who are different than me, and I don't want to foolishly fight against them when it is not a worthwhile fight. Help me to see from your perspective.

ABUNDANCE

God is able to make every grace overflow to you, so that in every way, always having everything you need, you may excel in every good work.

2 CORINTHIANS 9:8 CSB

God is so very good. He offers not only the bare minimum of what we need but more, so that we can share what we have been given with others. As he does to us, so we do to others. We are able to generously share our lives, blessings, and resources with others because of the abundance of God's generosity with us.

When we look at what we have as a gift, with some to put to use and some to share with others, we can build practices of generous giving that become as natural as any habit in our lives. It is good for us to acknowledge the power of God's generosity in our own lives, so we don't lose sight of partnering with his purposes by living it out in our communities. What a blessing it is to give.

Generous God, thank you for the abundance of your gifts in my life. I am so very grateful for your faithfulness to me. I won't neglect the absolute honor of showing that same generosity as I share what I have with others so that they, too, might know the grace of your goodness.

MIGHTY POWER

The message of the cross is foolishness to those who are perishing, but to us who are being saved it is the power of God.

1 CORINTHIANS 1:18 NKJV

Though the message of the cross seems like utter nonsense to those who don't choose to walk in the ways of Christ, it is the power of God released within those who have been saved by grace. The wisdom of the world's systems is foolishness, but the ways of God's kingdom are astoundingly wise, pure, and good.

The systems of this world are faulty. Why would we put our hope in them? No matter how hard we try, we cannot solve the problems of the world and create peace between all people. When we focus instead on loving others, the power of God is released by his grace in our lives. Suddenly, what felt impossible to overcome in our own willpower is possible in the mercy of Christ. Let's focus, then, on following the ways of his kingdom, for they will never fail.

Lord Jesus, your ways may sound foolish to those who are set on making their own names memorable, but they are the embodiment of wisdom. When we can rest from striving for our place, we can actually come alive from a place of rooted love. How wonderful you are.

RECEIVING WITH THANKS

Everything created by God is good, and nothing is to be rejected if it is received with thanksgiving.

1 TIMOTHY 4:4 ESV

Though you may prefer one way of eating over another, there is no holier diet than another. When we stop moralizing what we put in our bodies, how we choose to dress them, and other superficial elements, we can focus on the things that actually matter.

Everything created by God is good. We don't have to live under the convictions of others. We can choose what we consume, for nothing is to be rejected if it is received with thanksgiving. Let's be thankful for what is available to us and reject the notion that what we eat either makes us more or less holy. We can choose freely, and that's the point! If you don't like certain things, you don't have to choose those things. Let's receive with thanksgiving and release our need to weigh in on what others choose for themselves.

Lord, thank you for the freedom I have in you to choose what I consume and what I don't. I'm grateful for this, and I don't want to fall in the trap of moralizing anyone's eating habits. Help me to be grounded and covered in your love and focused on the things that truly matter.

REFINING FIRES

In every way we show we are servants of God:
in accepting many hard things, in troubles,
in difficulties, and in great problems.

2 CORINTHIANS 6:4 NCV

Difficult times can reveal our character in ways that peaceful times cannot. When we learn to accept hard things without running away from them, we show that we have strength and perseverance. Romans 5:3-4 says, "We also have joy with our troubles, because we know that these troubles produce patience… patience produces character, and character produces hope."

When problems arise in our lives, it is an opportunity to press in with patient endurance, which builds our character. It is a chance to really hold onto hope in practical ways. The Holy Spirit is our help in this. He offers us true love, patience, peace, kindness, and joy. He is our generous grace, our persistent help, in times of trouble. No problem lasts forever, so let's not let our hardships define our perspectives. Let's allow, instead, our perspectives to empower us in our hardships.

Holy Spirit, thank you for the power of your presence that produces the fruit of your kingdom in my life as much under pressure as not. I yield to your leadership through it all. May difficulties only cause me to become more like you.

EASY TO DISCOVER

He has done this so that every person would long for God,
feel their way to him, and find him—for he is the God
who is easy to discover!

ACTS 17:27 TPT

God is not far from each one of us. He is so very easy to
discover. Through time and history, he set the boundaries
of people and nations, putting us in our appointed times.
He has put a longing in each of us to discover his truth: the
truth of our inception and the enormity of his love.

Consider how you most easily connect to God and can see
his fingerprints. Is it in the natural world: a walk in nature,
stargazing on a dark, cold night, or looking over great waters
that seem to never end? Whatever causes awe to spark in
your heart and turns your thoughts to your Creator, spend
time doing that today. Remember, he is easy to discover.
Even right where you are in this very moment.

Wonderful One, thank you for making yourself so easy to
find. You don't hide in an obscure place that I may or may
not stumble upon. You are close to me even now. Open my
eyes to your presence.

SEASONED WITH GRACE

Let your conversation be always full of grace, seasoned with salt, so that you may know how to answer everyone.
COLOSSIANS 4:6 NIV

When we drench our conversations in grace, we make room for the truth and clarity of God's Word to break through. Whomever we are speaking to, whether they are followers of Jesus, atheists, or from another religious tradition, it should not affect how we speak with them. We are to be always full of grace in our conversations.

Grace does not limit the parameters of conversation with a strict agenda. It allows room for true heart-to-hearts. It makes space with humility, kindness, and generosity. It does not pull back from the truth, but it also has no need to hammer it down. Those who are gracious are able to be flexible in their reactions and approaches, knowing how to answer many different kinds of questions.

Gracious God, help me to keep every conversation seasoned with grace, that I may resist the urge to debate my own ideas for the sake of being heard. More than I want to be known as right, I want to be loving.

REFRESHING PERSPECTIVES

Let my teaching fall on you like rain;
let my speech settle like dew.
Let my words fall like rain on tender grass,
like gentle showers on young plants.

DEUTERONOMY 32:2 NLT

The teaching of the Lord's ways should not come down hard and fast, as an anvil falling from the sky. It is more like a gentle rain and dew that gathers and refreshes the hearer. The Lord's kindness leads us to repentance, not his anger.

This truth can change the way we relate to others. It's not that we will never lose our cool. We are still human, after all. However, when gracious kindness becomes our intention in our interactions, the truth can shine through in all of its power. Proverbs 16:24 says, "Kind words are like honey—sweet to the soul and healthy for the body." Kind does not mean disingenuous. True kindness comes from a heart that is grounded in the love and truth of God.

Kind Father, though the world may see kindness as weakness, I know it is actually strength. I want to reflect your tenderness, even as I speak the truth. May I learn the beauty and power of gentle truth-telling.

SHARPENED BY WISDOM

If the axe is dull and he does not sharpen its edge,
then he must exert more strength.
Wisdom has the advantage of giving success.

ECCLESIASTES 10:10 NASB

Wisdom sharpens our minds, our awareness, and our actions. It is a benefit to us when we allow the blade of God's wisdom to sharpen our own understanding. When we do, there is less of our own strength to exert.

Hebrews 4:12 describes the wisdom of God in this way: "The word of God is living and active, and sharper than any two-edged sword, even penetrating as far as the division of soul and spirit, of both joints and marrow, and able to judge the thoughts and intentions of the heart." Why would we rely on our own intellect when the wisdom of God provides sharper insights? We may be able to go so far, but God's perception takes us further.

Lord, I know that your wisdom is full of grace, truth, and power. I don't want to rely on my own limited understanding today. I welcome your wisdom, strategies, and the power of your perspective in every area of my life.

EVERY SINGLE DAY

Encourage each other daily, while it is still called today,
so that none of you is hardened by sin's deception.
HEBREWS 3:13 CSB

Every day is an opportunity to encourage the people in our lives. As we lean on each other, we can continue to support and inspire one another to remain humble in God's love, open to his wisdom and correction, and reach out for help when we need it.

We need the support of each other in life. We are relational beings, and we become like those we most spend our time with. As we remain cognizant of who we are influenced by and whom we are pouring into, it is important that we not forget the importance of encouragement. Perhaps there are some people we need to spend less time with. Maybe we need more connection with those who are heading in the same direction we want to go. Every day is an opportunity to reflect, connect, and choose how we will live, as well as whom we do life with.

Present One, thank you for the people in my life who are living examples of your love and truth. I do not take them for granted. As I go about my day, show me ways I can offer encouragement to those around me, as well as what I can receive from them.

SPRINGS OF LIFE

"Behold, I am doing a new thing;
now it springs forth, do you not perceive it?
I will make a way in the wilderness
and rivers in the desert."

ISAIAH 43:19 ESV

The mercy of God never grows stale. It is not stagnant or unrelatable. It is always moving, always fresh, and always breeding new life. What new thing is God doing? Ask him for eyes to see what he has begun to birth in you. Perhaps you already have an idea of what it is. He makes ways in the wilderness and springs in the desert. What barren areas have begun to show signs of life? God is doing a new thing.

As you consider the power of God's mercy in your life, write out a prayer of thanks. Be specific and clear. Thank him for what he has done, what he has brought you through, and what he is starting to do even now. He is marvelous in mercy, and he is abundant in redemption life. Now it springs forth, do you not perceive it?

Redeemer, I'm so grateful that there is always newness in you. No matter how many ends I face in this life, there are always new beginnings right there. Thank you.

LET HIM DO IT

Humble yourselves in the sight of the Lord,
and he will lift you up.
JAMES 4:10 NKJV

When you feel the pain of your mistakes, don't just try to escape it. In the presence of the Lord, allow yourself to feel the pain. Cry if you must. Be sad. It's not less holy to feel your sorrow. In fact, in order to fully get through your pain, you must allow yourself first to feel it. Weep for the regret.

And then, when you have laid yourself humble before the Lord, he will lift you up. When you are willing to recognize the weak areas of your life, the places where you failed, you can rightly present yourself before God. He will not shame you or punish you. No, he lifts you up in love and restores you in kindness. He removes the weight of your sin and frees you to choose differently. Feel the pain, and then let God do the work of raising you up and out of it.

Lord, thank you for the power of your mercy that heals, restores, and redeems. I won't try to escape sorrow when it settles in, and I won't try to run away from the pain of regret. I know I have to feel it to move through it. Help me, Lord, and lift me up in my weakness.

MAKE A CHANGE

"Change your hearts and lives
because the kingdom of heaven is near."
MATTHEW 3:2 NCV

John the Baptist prepared the people's hearts for the ministry of Jesus. The invitation to change our hearts and lives remains as poignant today, for the kingdom of heaven is near to us now through Christ.

Let's not put off for another day the changes we want to make in our lives. If we want to spend more time with our families, then we can take steps to do that now. If we want to improve our health, then there are meaningful choices we can make that will help us. If we have been putting off putting Christ first in our lives for when it feels more convenient, today is the day to change our priorities. God honors every step we make toward him and toward our freedom. The kingdom of heaven is near, so we must not delay.

Jesus Christ, you are my Savior and the one I put above all else. Show me areas that I have been putting off making meaningful changes that need to be done. Help me to take those steps today.

EVERY DETAIL

"Don't worry. For your Father cares deeply
about even the smallest detail of your life."
MATTHEW 10:30 TPT

God doesn't overlook any part of our lives. He cares deeply
about even the smallest detail of your life. Let that sink
in. Those seemingly insignificant things that capture your
attention? God cares about them. If you have any worries
today, no matter whether they are big or small, God can be
trusted to take care of them.

Whether or not you consider yourself to be a detail-oriented
person, God is. He doesn't miss anything. He doesn't forget
even the things that slip your mind. You don't have to worry.
He covers the cracks with his overpowering mercy. Trust
him with the details. You may not know how things will
work out, but he does. They will. Trust him.

Faithful Father, another day and yet another invitation to
give you my worries. I don't want to be consumed with the
unknowns of things I cannot answer. I trust you to take
care of me, in both big and little ways. I believe that you are
trustworthy and true. Thank you.

CULTIVATING LOVE

Whoever would foster love covers over an offense,
but whoever repeats the matter separates close friends.
PROVERBS 17:9 NIV

Love does not look for reasons to hold grudges. It doesn't
dwell on others' mistakes. Love chooses to overlook the
mistakes of others. What generosity there is in this. What
opportunity for peace in our relationships.

Proverbs 19:11 says, "It is to one's glory to overlook an
offense." It is easier to overlook the faults of those we love
than it is those we don't have relationship with. As we
cultivate love in our hearts for those in our lives, we build
our own ability to overlook the offenses of others. This isn't
the same thing as suffering under abuse. We don't have
to submit ourselves to people who continually hurt us in
the same ways over and over again—that is not loving for
either them or us. Cultivating love includes loving ourselves
enough to let go of the need for others to be perfect. This
love releases grace, peace, and intimacy.

Loving God, there isn't anyone who overlooks more
faults than you do. As I foster love in my own heart and
relationships, help me to choose to let go of the minor
things that don't matter. Thank you.

HIDE IN HIM

You are my hiding place;
you protect me from trouble.
You surround me with songs of victory.
PSALM 32:7 NLT

If you feel the urge to hide at all, hide yourself in the canopy of God's presence. He will protect you from trouble, and he will surround you with the songs of his victory. His presence is full of perfect peace, stable wisdom, and uplifting hope. He calms anxious hearts and watches over the vulnerable.

Run into the shelter of God's love when your feet are ready to race from your circumstances. Even if you physically don't move a muscle, your heart and soul can find rest in the presence of his peace. He is near. Bring him every care, every worry, and every question you have. You can bring your baggage with you, for he will exchange his light load for them. It's okay to run and hide, if you need to, but run and hide in your God, for he is a safe place of shelter.

Victorious One, you are my hiding place. I come to you whenever my heart needs a place to take shelter. Thank you for faithfully protecting me in your love. You are my strong foundation, and I won't run from you.

TASTE AND SEE

Taste and see that the LORD is good;
how blessed is the man who takes refuge in him!
PSALM 34:8 NASB

The Lord is good. This is a truth that always remains. If it has been a while since you tasted his goodness, come and feast on his presence. If you have not recognized the loving-kindness of God in your own life, then consider this your invitation.

Blessed is the man who takes refuge in him. Blessed are you when you run to hide in the shelter of God's love. He is a safe place at all times, in every way. You will taste the goodness of the Lord. You will see how wonderful he is toward you. As David prayed, so can you: "I certainly believed that I would see the goodness of the Lord in the land of the living" (Psalm 27:13). Believe it, still, beloved. As long as you draw breath into your lungs, the goodness of God is near.

Good Father, you are exceedingly good to all who look to you for help. I won't stop coming to you over and over again with the hunger in my heart. I want to taste and see your goodness in fresh and new ways today. Thank you that I will.

CHOOSING EMPATHY

Rejoice with those who rejoice;
weep with those who weep.

ROMANS 12:15 CSB

It is love that meets someone's sorrow with our own compassion. It is kind-heartedness that joins in celebration with those who have reason to rejoice. When we are mindful of each other, both of our differing experiences and also our shared worth, we learn to step back from our own priorities for a time and put others first.

Is it hard for you to celebrate with those who have experienced a tremendous breakthrough in their lives? Is it difficult for you to step into someone's pain with them? If so, you may need to practice growing your capacity for empathy. Empathy does not only seek to understand someone else's perspective, but it also responds to it in kind. God does this with us all the time. He meets us where we are at, speaking to us in ways that are extremely poignant for where we are at in the moment. May we learn to be more like him with others.

Merciful Father, thank you for the power of your love that rejoices with those who celebrate and for weeping with those who weep. I have known the power of empathy in my own life, and I choose to grow in it in relation to those around me.

PREPARE AND TRUST

The horse is made ready for the day of battle,
but the victory belongs to the LORD.
PROVERBS 21:31 ESV

It would be foolish for an army to neglect preparations for a battle they knew was coming. Foresight offers us wisdom in how we can prepare for what lies ahead. We don't know how the tides of battle will turn, but we bring ourselves to the battlefield as ready as we can be.

The victory belongs to the Lord. As you partner with him, you can trust that no matter what happens, he will reign through it all. Rely on the Lord, for no matter how outnumbered you feel, his power is unmatched. Follow his directives and his leadership, for he won't lead you astray. Make preparations and trust God.

God, you are the victorious one who reigns over all. In you, I find peace, hope, and strength. I will not ignore what is mine to do today, even as I know that I can't predict the future. I will prepare the best way I know how, and I will trust the rest to you.

LIVING FOR GOODNESS

Seek good and not evil,
that you may live;
so the LORD God of hosts will be with you,
as you have spoken.

AMOS 5:14 NKJV

If we want to know the goodness that God calls us to seek through our lived-out actions, then we have only to look through Scripture. "For all the law is fulfilled in one word, even in this: "You shall love your neighbor as yourself" (Galatians 5:14). When you learn to love and consider others the same way you love and consider yourself, you are seeking the good that today's verse speaks of.

There is renewal for us as we walk in the ways of Christ. There is hope and help for us in the presence of God as we do. He is always close at hand, and his leadership does not disappoint or fail us. It is always better to seek to do good to others, for it will echo back to us every time we do. Generosity of heart is always rewarded.

Mighty God, I want to be known as one who considers others as often as I do myself. I want to love well, to do good, and to pursue peace. Thank you for your grace, your strength, and your empowering love as I do.

ALL THE TIME

"I am a God who is near," says the LORD.
"I am also a God who is far away.
No one can hide where I cannot see him," says the LORD.
"I fill all of heaven and earth," says the LORD.

JEREMIAH 23:23-24 NCV

The Lord God cannot be contained, and he cannot be pinned down. He is both near and far. He is vast and palpable. His presence is everywhere, for he is Spirit. He fills all of heaven and earth. Beyond our greatest imaginings, God exists even greater still.

With this in mind, let's allow our own expectations of God, his power, and his goodness to grow in kind. We need not put limits on his being in order to alleviate our expectations. He exists far outside our scope of humanity. He is not bound by the things that bind us. He is so much greater! Take hope in this one who is near, and to this one who is simultaneously far away. His power no one can fathom.

Inescapable One, you cannot be pinned down. I don't want to dumb you down to my level. I want to transform in the grandiosity of who you are. May the expectations of my faith grow even as my imagination stretches to know you more.

STILL REJOICING

We may suffer, yet in every season we are always found rejoicing. We may be poor, yet we bestow great riches on many. We seem to have nothing, yet in reality we possess all things.

2 CORINTHIANS 6:10 TPT

When you go through hard seasons where the suffering is long and the pain is deep, may you still be found rejoicing in the goodness of your God. No matter how little you may have to your name, there is still much that you can offer others. Even when it seems as if you have nothing the world values, you have riches in the kingdom of Christ, for you have God as your Savior, your Father, and your Friend.

What greater reason to rejoice is there than knowing that you are loved by the King of kings and Lord of lords? No matter what season you are in, look for the light that still shines through: the pure light of God's love. It is as close as it ever was. There are pockets of peace and moments of miraculous mercy. You are filled with the abundance of Christ, here and now.

Lord, may I still be found rejoicing, even in suffering. You are my goodness, my present peace, and my reason to celebrate in every season. I love you so.

FULL OF COMPASSION

Praise be to the God and Father of our Lord Jesus Christ,
the Father of compassion and the God of all comfort.

2 CORINTHIANS 1:3 NIV

God is the Father of compassion. He is the God of all
comfort. When we are heartbroken, he is near. He knows us
just as we are; he sees our weaknesses, and he reads the pain
of our hearts. We are not a mystery to him, even when we
can't figure out our own distress.

There is no need to hide how you're really feeling from the
Lord today. He already knows. You don't have to dress it up
or pretend that you are fine when you are not. He does not
want your best self. He just wants you. Allow him to minister
to the parts of you that so desperately need his compassion
and comfort. In him, your soul can find rest, refreshment,
and relief.

Compassionate Father, I don't know why I try to hide my
pain from you. You already know it well. I receive your
comfort and compassion today. Lift the weight of my
burdens with the comfort of your presence, Lord.

GREAT EXPECTATION

It is by his great mercy that we have been born again. Now we live with great expectation, and we have a priceless inheritance—an inheritance that is kept in heaven for you, pure and undefiled, beyond the reach of change and decay.

1 PETER 1:3-4 NLT

In the incredible mercy of Christ, we experience renewal and transformation. He breathes life into our souls as if we were dead and now we are alive. Every good thing comes from the Father. Every perfect gift is from his hand. Every act of pure love reflects his own. May we look for the fingerprints of his mercy in the world around us, for he is alive and moving in our midst.

We have great expectations, not only for eternal life in his kingdom, but also for the lives we live in him now. There is hope in him, and there is comfort in his presence. There is joy in his transformative power, and there is overwhelming confidence in his faithfulness. He never stops moving in pure love, and he never will. Though we only get glimpses of his glory now, one day we will see it fully. What great expectations we have!

Glorious God, there is no one greater than you. All of my hopes are set on you. I trust that your love will never fail. Even when I falter, you are faithful. I worship you.

ALWAYS A WAY

No temptation has overtaken you except something
common to mankind; and God is faithful, so he will not
allow you to be tempted beyond what you are able, but with
the temptation will provide the way of escape also, so that
you will be able to endure it.

1 CORINTHIANS 10:13 NASB

Have you ever felt completely powerless to temptation? No
matter what it is, you always have a choice. Jesus spent forty
days in the wilderness being tempted in every way, yet he
withstood each and every one. He remained strong in faith
and refused to trade his relationship with the Father for
something that would never satisfy.

Even if you have fallen a thousand times, you can still choose
a different way today. Temptations are common, but God
is faithful. There's always a way to stand up under it. Jesus,
your Savior and companion, will help you with his faithful
presence. The Spirit offers grace-strength to choose the
better way. And when you fall, fall into the arms of grace and
don't allow shame to keep you from rising up again.

Righteous One, in your victory, I find victory. I trust you
to help me when I am tempted to choose another way than
your love. Thank you for your help and for your redemption.

JUST A SHADOW

"Who am I, and who are my people, that we should be able
to give as generously as this? For everything comes from
you, and we have given you only what comes from your own
hand. For we are aliens and temporary residents in your
presence as were all our ancestors. Our days on earth are like
a shadow, without hope."

1 CHRONICLES 29:14-15 CSB

Even though are lives are but shadows that are here one
moment and gone the next, God cares for us as his own
children. We can offer God the honest response of our hearts
to him in worship. All things come from him. All that we
offer him back originally was his to begin with.

God does not leave us in our weakness or in our wallowing.
When we embrace the insignificance we feel, we can also
embrace the power of his love for us at the same time. David
said it this way in Psalm 8:4, "What are human beings that
you are mindful of them, mortals that you care for them?"
God gives us our worth by caring for us unequivocally. It is
almost too much to comprehend. Even though our lives are
like mist, God delights in them, in us, just the same.

Almighty God, thank you for all that you have given me. I offer
it right back to you in gratitude. Thank you for loving me. I
can't help but love you, for you are incredibly good to me.

ABIDE IN TRUTH

His anointing teaches you about everything, and is true,
and is no lie—just as it has taught you, abide in him.
1 JOHN 2:27 ESV

The anointing is not some mysterious thing that some get
and some don't. What John is speaking of when he says "his
anointing teaches you" is the Holy Spirit. The anointing
of the Spirit brings life, illumination, the fruit of Christ's
kingdom, power, and wisdom. He teaches us the truth, and
he reveals the ways of God to our hearts.

Abide in the Holy Spirit, making your home in him just
as surely as he has made his home in you. Commune with
him in the secret place of your soul. Open yourself to his
leadership in your life. The ways of God are revealed through
his fellowship, and the fruit of his work in your life are
always the fruit described in Galatians five. Trust him, be at
home in him, and cultivate your relationship with him. He is
always near.

Holy Spirit, you are the anointing of God that teaches me
to walk in the wisdom and ways of Christ. I submit to your
leadership, and I partner with your purposes. Be at home in
me, even as I find myself at home in you.

DECEMBER

When the Spirit of truth comes, he
will guide you into all truth, for he
will not speak on his own authority,
but whatever he hears he will speak,
and he will declare to you the
things that are to come.

JOHN 16:13 ESV

STAY THE COURSE

Do not turn aside; for then you would go after empty things
which cannot profit or deliver, for they are nothing.

1 SAMUEL 12:21 NKJV

When we shift off-course from walking in the ways of God,
we will become distracted by things that don't profit us.
When we remain rooted and grounded in the nature of God,
following his leadership and living out the qualities of his
kingdom, we will benefit from the purity and power of his
life in our own.

Take some time to consider what are the things you are
pursuing right now. It could be the favor of friends, a new
promotion, or a balance in life. None of these things are
wrong. Now consider how you are going about pursuing
them. If it is not in the integrity of God's ways, then you
may have some readjusting to do. Ask the Spirit to show you
where you can align in the fruit of God's kingdom as you
pursue the full expression of his love in your life.

Lord, no matter where I go or what I do, you are at the
center of it all. Where I have cut corners or lost sight of what
is important, open my eyes. I don't want to go after empty
things; but rather, remain with my vision on the fullness of
who you are and who I am in you.

SENT TO SAVE

"God did not send his Son into the world to judge the world guilty, but to save the world through him."

JOHN 3:17 NCV

When we share the message of Christ's life, death, and resurrection, the focus should be on salvation, not on judgment. For God did not send his Son to judge the world guilty. He sent him to save the world through him. When we uplift messages of judgment over grace, we miss the point of the gospel altogether.

Jesus quoted Isaiah when he said, "The Lord has put his Spirit in me, because he appointed me to tell the Good News to the poor. He has sent me to tell the captives they are free and to tell the blind that they can see again. God sent me to free those who have been treated unfairly" (Luke 4:18). If the gospel we preach and ascribe to isn't good news to the poor, the captive, and the abused, then it is not the full gospel of Christ.

Savior, thank you for the power of your love that sets the captive free and gives sight to the blind. You are exceedingly good. May I know you in this way. May I always point to you in this way, as well. You are the Redeemer we all need.

CONFIDENCE IN CRISIS

God is your confidence in times of crisis,
keeping your heart at rest in every situation.
PROVERBS 3:26 TPT

There is no moment in our lives or on the earth where the peace of God is not available to us. Jesus said it this way: "I leave the gift of peace… not the kind of fragile peace given by the world… don't yield to fear or be troubled in your hearts" (John 14:27). The peace of God permeates our hearts and minds, calming our nervous systems and the chaos of spinning thoughts. His presence always leads us to rest.

How can you hold onto God and the confidence of his faithfulness, even in times of crisis? As you cultivate deep friendship and reliance on his Spirit in times of calm, you build a bridge of trust that cannot be broken. Don't neglect the power of the relationship you have with the Lord. He is near, and he is faithful through every trial and triumph.

Faithful God, you give me rest, even in raging storms. You are my safe place, and I can never lose you. Thank you for being my confidence in every season and stage. I trust you.

COMPLETELY FAMILIAR

You discern my going out and my lying down;
you are familiar with all my ways.
Before a word is on my tongue,
you, Lord, know it completely.
You hem me in behind and before,
and you lay your hand upon me.

PSALM 139:3-5 NIV

The God who created you knows you better than anyone else. You are not a mystery to him. He loves you through and through, hemming you in behind and before, keeping watch over you. There is so much goodness, peace, and strength in choosing to follow his ways. He will not lead you astray, and he won't trick you.

You were created to know God, to become familiar with his ways. You were created for deep fellowship with your Father, Savior, and the Spirit of God. There isn't anything he lacks, even when you don't have a thing to your name. Trust him, love him, and spend time getting to know him more. Then you will find that there is no reason to fear or try to run from his presence. He is good, and he is compassionate toward all that he has made.

Lord, I am humbled to know that you know me and love me thoroughly. Why would I look for satisfaction apart from you? Your love is the fuel to my heart, my life, and my hope. I love you.

DIFFERENT EXPRESSIONS

God works in different ways,
but it is the same God who does the work in all of us.
1 CORINTHIANS 12:6 NLT

Our lives weren't meant to be mirror images of each other.
God works differently in each of us, and he has offered us
the clear fruit of his Spirit to know that it is not the outer
expression that matters, but what lies beneath that does. The
same God is at work in all who are yielded to him, without
exception. We can see this through the Spirit fruit that is
produced in our lives.

Instead of getting caught up on superficial spirituality, we
should look to grow the roots of our faith in the kingdom of
God. We may prefer different music, dress differently, have
a variety of jobs and hobbies, and not one of those things
accurately depicts our faith in Christ. It always comes down
to the fruit—always. Let's learn to delight in each other's
differences, even as we look for the beautiful ways that God
unites us in heart, purpose, and love.

God, thank you for the freedom I find in you. I don't have to
go to Bible school or pursue ministry in order to fully follow
you in my life. I follow the path you have laid out for me,
even if it feels like a lonely one. I trust you.

BRIDGES OF LOVE

Though you have not seen him, you love him, and though
you do not see him now, but believe in him, you greatly
rejoice with joy inexpressible and full of glory.

1 PETER 1:8 NASB

Love is a powerful force. It does not need to be nurtured
face-to-face, though it can help. You may never have known
your great-grandmother, but because of the stories passed
down, you love her. God is not distant from us, and it is not
simply through the accounts of Scripture or others that we
can love him. His Spirit works in our lives, causing our love
to grow exponentially.

When we recognize the work of God's mercy in our lives,
let's not be quick to overlook it. It can serve as a slab in the
foundation of our faith, strengthening what has already been
laid through the experiences of others. As we walk with him,
even though we do not see him, we know him. We come to
know the power of his presence, his peace, his joy, his love,
and his heart of justice. What an opportunity we have to
continue to experience the joy of his glorious goodness in
our lives, loving him more and more until we come face-to-
face with him in the fullness of his timing.

Lord, thank you for your presence, power, and glory.
I love you.

HE IS COMING

"Sing and rejoice, O daughter of Zion! For behold, I am coming and I will dwell in your midst," says the LORD. "Many nations shall be joined to the LORD in that day, and they shall become my people. And I will dwell in your midst. Then you will know that the LORD of hosts has sent me to you."

ZECHARIAH 2:10-11 NKJV

We are still waiting to experience the fullness of God's kingdom. He promises that he will wipe every tear from our eyes, and the pain of death will be but a memory. We will be united with his sons and daughters from every tribe, nation, and language. Until that day, we wait with hope.

As we wait, we have the power of Christ's resurrection as our own triumph. We have been brought close to God in his mercy, with every accusation against us silenced in the power of his love. We have been purified, redeemed, and liberated. Let's not lose sight of the hope of our calling, for God is with us now in Spirit until we dwell with him in the fullness of his promise.

King Jesus, I am so grateful for glimpses of your glorious kingdom in this world and in my life. I wait with hope for the day that you will reign fully and completely and silence every other competing voice.

BELIEVE IT

"I tell you, whatever you ask in prayer,
believe that you have received it,
and it will be yours."

MARK 11:24 ESV

You are welcomed into God's presence with open arms whenever you approach him. Don't hesitate to pour out your heart to him. Pray, and when you do, believe that God hears you and honors the requests of your heart.

Cultivate your faith as you press into growing your prayer life. As you pray, do it boldly and without apology. Your God is a good Father, and he loves to delight in you. He hears your succinct prayers, as well as your ramblings. You don't have to wonder whether he wants to take the time to listen to you. He always has time for you. As you pray today, stretch your own faith as you do, and believe that what you have asked for, you have received it. And receive it with gratitude.

Faithful Lord, I want my faith to grow in the power of your love. As I stretch myself to ask for what I need and long for, I trust you to provide it. Thank you.

OVERFLOWING

"Blessed are those who hunger and thirst for righteousness,
for they will be filled."

MATTHEW 5:6 CSB

When we hunger and thirst for the goodness of God and for his righteousness, we will be satisfied. For he gives grain to the hungry and water to the thirsty soul. He does not ignore our hunger. He honors it, offering the spiritual food that truly nourishes and satisfies us.

The Lord is overwhelmingly abundant in righteousness. It is who he is. In Christ, we are covered fully by his mercy and goodness. 2 Corinthians 5:21 says, "For our sake he made him to be sin who knew no sin, so that in him we might become the righteousness of God." If we have become the righteousness of God, then we hunger and thirst no more. We live from the satisfaction of Christ's life within our own. What a glorious reality this is.

Righteous One, though I lacked in righteousness on my own, you gave me your own. Thank you for satisfying my hunger and thirst with the abundance of your goodness and mercy. As I draw upon your overflowing nature, I can live freely as an expression of your kindness.

HAPPY TO HOST

The believers met together in the Temple every day.
They ate together in their homes,
happy to share their food with joyful hearts.

ACTS 2:46 NCV

Though we may not be able to meet together with other believers every day, we can certainly host each other in ordinary times. We were created for community and connection, and that can only grow as we regularly see each other. We should not neglect the power of building connection as we host one another in our homes and share meals together.

When was the last time you met other believers outside of a church meeting or building in order to foster fellowship? Even if you don't have space to host a group of people, can you be creative in getting together with one or two others in your ordinary life? Perhaps you can meet at a restaurant, go for a walk, or have them over for coffee or tea. It is so important to spend time together, so in whatever ways you can, take the step of reaching out and fostering that connection in your day-to-day life.

Father, thank you for the gift of community and connection, of friendship and support. Help me to find creative ways to connect with others, even if it does not come naturally to me. Thank you.

MINISTRY OF RECONCILIATION

God has made all things new, and reconciled us to himself,
and given us the ministry of reconciling others to God.
2 CORINTHIANS 5:18 TPT

In Christ, we have been made new. We have been restored
to what we were always meant for: friendship with God. As
children of God, we get to partner with him in offering that
same restoration to others. Everyone is made in the image
of God, and through Christ, they are able to have friendship
with him.

God is a perfect friend; he does not compete with us or lord
over us the ways that we fail to meet his expectations. In fact,
he has no delusions of our identity. He knows us well, and
he accepts us in compassion. He transforms our hearts and
minds in his wisdom and by his Spirit. He always has time
for us. What wonderful news! Do you know someone who
desperately needs a friend? Point them in the direction of the
one who will never, ever fail them. This is how you partner
with God in the ministry of reconciliation.

Redeemer, thank you for making all things new including
me. You are better than the best of friends. Your motives are
pure and your heart kind. I will partner with your purposes
and share your goodness with others.

ALWAYS IN SIGHT

I keep my eyes always on the LORD.
With him at my right hand, I will not be shaken.
Therefore my heart is glad and my tongue rejoices;
my body also will rest secure.

PSALM 16:8-9 NIV

Every day is a fresh chance to fix your eyes on the Lord. He is always near, always within sight. No matter what you walk into today, go with the confidence that God is at your right hand. He goes with you. Don't let others intimidate you, for you already know who you are. Perhaps you need a refresher. Let the Spirit of God speak his truth about your identity over you even now.

With joy in your heart in knowing that you are completely loved, may you be empowered to walk courageously and boldly into any and every room. You are not behind in life, and you are not lacking in anything. You have all that you need in the presence of the Lord and in his companionship. Keep your eyes on him and walk with your head held high.

Lord, thank you for reminding me of my worth, and that it is always and truly rooted in you. I won't be afraid of what others think. You are my confidence, today and always.

IN SPIRIT AND TRUTH

"The time is coming—indeed it's here now—when true worshipers will worship the Father in spirit and in truth. The Father is looking for those who will worship him that way."

JOHN 4:23 NLT

We are not called to worship God in flattery or in superficiality. He doesn't need us to throw empty words his way. We worship him in spirit and in truth when we live according to his law of love. When we offer him the trust of our hearts and decisions, whether we are gathered with others in his name or completely alone, we honor him.

God wants our sincerity, not lip service. He is not afraid of the questions we have or the range of our emotions. He is an emotional God; after all, we were created in his image. So worship God today, not because you feel obligated to, but in the sincerity of your heart. It does not need to be in song or prayer. It can be as simple as doing the right thing when it is presented.

Jesus, I worship you in spirit and truth, whatever form that takes in my lived-out day. I know you see my heart, and I don't have to explain myself to you. Thank you for honoring my sincere worship.

SONS AND DAUGHTERS

"I will be a father to you, and you shall be sons and
daughters to me," says the Lord Almighty.

2 CORINTHIANS 6:18 NASB

In Christ, we have been adopted into the family of God.
We are his sons and daughters. Knowing this, we can freely
come to him anytime, anywhere, in any circumstance. He
welcomes us, not as strangers, but as family.

Even as you get ready to gather with loved ones around the
holidays, with all the mixed feelings that may be present,
your heavenly Father awaits your fellowship. He is a perfect
Father. He does not misunderstand you or misrepresent
you. He is not disappointed in you. He loves you, he loves
spending time with you, and he delights in every shared
moment. When your earthly family misses the mark, he
never does. Take time today and throughout the busy
holidays to fellowship with your good Father, you faithful
friend, and your close comfort.

Father, thank you for being the perfect parent. I trust you to
receive me with love every time I turn to you. Thank you for
being kind, even in your correction. I love you.

MORE THAN ABLE

He himself has suffered when he was tempted,
he is able to help those who are tempted.
HEBREWS 2:18 CSB

Jesus knew weakness in his human body. He knows what it feels like to be utterly exhausted, hungry, and annoyed. He was tempted, he suffered loss, and he persevered in love, devotion, and hope.

Whatever complicated feelings you experience, Jesus gets it. He himself suffered loss of relationship, he knew what it was to grieve the death of loved ones, and he was unjustly persecuted for his values. Lean into his help when you yourself are in the refining fires of life. He will not turn you away. He will help you to overcome the weight of what threatens to crush you. He will not let you be destroyed. Go to him; he knows what you are going through, and he is more than able to empower you in the midst of it.

Lord Jesus, thank you for already walking the path of testing and for relating to us in our humanity. I trust that your help is sufficient. Give me grace in your fellowship as I walk through hard times. You are the one I lean on more than any other.

PRECIOUS PROMISES

He has granted to us his precious and very great promises,
so that through them you may become partakers of the
divine nature, having escaped from the corruption
that is in the world because of sinful desire.

2 PETER 1:4 ESV

Through the promise of Christ, we are able to partner with his divine nature to experience triumph over sin. His mercy covers us completely, and we are liberated in his love to live as lights of his glorious goodness in this world.

If we are in Christ, we are free. We are not bound by fear, shame, sin, or death. In the kingdom of God, where his promises are fully developed, we put our hope and confidence. Though we may suffer a little now in this life, we will one day be free from pain. Though we may experience the chaos of corruption in this world, God remains our peace. There is no problem he won't fix, and there's no mountain that can't be moved in his power. Let's align our hearts, our choices, and our lives in the living love of Christ that conquers fear.

Jesus Christ, I believe that you are the way, you are the truth, and you are the life. I am yours, and I cling to your promises like they are my daily nourishment. May I come even more alive, free, and hopeful in your love today.

DEDICATED TO GOD

"For this child I prayed, and the LORD has granted me my petition which I asked of him. Therefore I also have lent him to the LORD; as long as he lives he shall be lent to the LORD."

1 SAMUEL 1:27-28 NKJV

When the Lord answers our prayers, what is our response to him? Instead of simply moving on, quickly forgetting both the longing and the poignant provision of God, let's remember that each answer to prayer is a gift from God. We can hold them loosely before the Lord who offered us his palpable mercy, dedicating even the answer to our prayers back to him.

Every good gift in this life is from the Father of lights (James 1:17). Every perfect gift is from his hand. Recognizing the source of the goodness in our lives, we can offer it back to him as an offering. As we do, we keep our hearts open, while honoring the Lord and his hand of mercy in our lives.

Gracious God, thank you for the good and perfect gifts of your love in my life. Thank you for answering the longings of my heart with your provision. They were, are, and remain, yours.

EVEN MORE STRENGTH

He gives strength to those who are tired
and more power to those who are weak.

ISAIAH 40:29 NCV

When we are tired, God gives us strength. When we are weak, he offers us more power. It is as simple as that. The Word of God does not say that those who walk in the ways of the Lord will never tire or grow weary. We do, in fact, tire easily. He offers us rest when we are worn down. He leads us beside still waters to restore our souls.

No matter how tired you are today, God has grace-strength to empower you. He has power for your weakness. Lean into his presence and ask him for his help. You don't have to power through on your own. He has more than enough strength to help you in your weariness. And don't resist rest. It is in the places of rest where we are refreshed, restored, and rejuvenated time and again.

Mighty One, thank you for not demanding strength from me. You accept me in my weakness, offering me your own grace. I rest in you, and I receive your power in the place of my weakness. Thank you.

FREE FROM WORRY

The work of righteousness is peace, and the result of righteousness is quietness and confidence forever. My people will live free from worry in secure, quiet resting places.

ISAIAH 32:17-18 TPT

The work of righteousness does not sow dissension but peace. The result of righteousness is not chaos and insecurity but quietness and confidence. If we walk in the ways of righteousness, this is how we will be known: as pursuers of peace. We will be recognized as reliable in discernment that produces humble confidence.

Even if the world around us is chaotic, we can live in quiet homes of peace. We can cultivate homes that are secure in the love of God, living free from the weight of worries. It's not that our homes will never know challenges, but we can still know peace through them. The palpable peace of God is the atmosphere of his presence, so anywhere he is, we can also know security and peace.

Prince of Peace, I want to be known as a pursuer of peace rather than a stirrer of chaos. You are good, and that is always true. You are faithful, and I want to live in the security of your faithfulness all my days. May my home reflect your peace, where all can lay down their worries and burdens and truly rest.

GENERATIONS OF FAITHFULNESS

"The LORD is my strength and my defense;
he has become my salvation.
He is my God, and I will praise him,
my father's God, and I will exalt him."

EXODUS 15:2 NIV

God is faithful through all generations. He is not only present in the past, and he is not relegated to the present. His power is palpable throughout the ages, and he won't ever stop moving in loyal love to all who look to him. If you need a reminder of the power of God, look to the testimonies of those who have come before. Ask older generations about their experience. Think of your own encounters with his goodness.

Just as the Faithful One was God to Abraham, Moses, and David, we can call him "my God," as well. He is as present with us as he was with them. His presence is near, and we have the Holy Spirit at all times, in all circumstances. May our hope and faith grow as we remember the testimonies of his goodness to all generations including our own.

Faithful One, there is no one like you in all the universe. You are always my strength and my defense. You are my salvation. I trust you. May my heart grow in confidence as I see you in history, as well as the present.

BROUGHT NEAR

You have been united with Christ Jesus. Once you were far away from God, but now you have been brought near to him through the blood of Christ.

EPHESIANS 2:13 NLT

The blood of Christ is like a bridge. It connects us to God the Father directly. We can come boldly into his presence without fear because Christ has done all that was necessary to be united in peace with God.

You are not far away from God, no matter how distant he feels. Turn your heart toward Christ, and you will find that he is nearer than your very breath. You have been brought near to God, the creator of the universe, through Christ. Don't keep yourself at a distance for fear of what his reception may be of you. Read through the parable of the prodigal son, if you need a reminder of the Father's heart toward you. He is overflowing in affection for you at all times. Come to him without restraint, for he is your home, and he will restore even the dignity you feel you have lost.

Lord Jesus, thank you for the power of your blood that acts as a bridge to bring me close to the Father. Thank you for doing all that was necessary to restore me to the Father's love. I yield to your love today, knowing it is my source and strength, and my redemption.

LIVING HOPE

Blessed be the God and Father of our Lord Jesus Christ, who according to his great mercy has caused us to be born again to a living hope through the resurrection of Jesus Christ from the dead.

1 PETER 1:3 NASB

We have a living hope, not a far-off dream that fails to come to fruition. Jesus Christ is our embodied hope, and he is alive and still moving in the earth. His short life was not the end of the story. He resurrected from the grave, going to live with the Father and to intercede on our behalf until the fullness of timing calls him back.

Through Christ, we have been born again. We have been made new in the mercy of his life within us. The Spirit transforms us from the inside out, and the wisdom of God leads us through the hills and valleys of this life. Through it all, our living hope remains, and it will not be extinguished by the chaos of this world.

Faithful Father, I set the attention of my heart and mind on my living hope: Christ with me. Thank you for ministering to my heart in radiant joy and delight as your Spirit moves within. I am yours.

BUILD THOSE MUSCLES

Be strengthened by the Lord
and by his vast strength.
EPHESIANS 6:10 CSB

We can strengthen our spiritual muscles as practically as we can our physical ones. Spiritual strength training takes discipline and consistency, as well as a lot of grace. The Holy Spirit is our trainer, helping us to grow in the power of his presence.

Diligence and focus are as necessary as the mercy and grace of God in growing in strength. We must learn to incorporate rhythms of rest, as well as intense periods of training. If we want to grow strong, we have to go beyond the limits of our comfort. We need to persevere, to keep our minds fixed on the goal, and to allow redirection when injured. Thankfully, we have so much grace in the presence of the Lord. As we partner with him, he moves in us. He knows us well, and he is not a harsh trainer. He is the wisest, kindest, most encouraging and motivating coach we could ever have.

Holy Spirit, thank you for your leadership and wisdom in my life. As I train to strengthen my heart, mind, body, and spirit in you and your ways, I yield to your leadership in all things.

WONDERFUL GOD

To us a child is born,
to us a son is given;
and the government shall be upon his shoulder,
and his name shall be called
Wonderful Counselor, Mighty God, Everlasting Father,
Prince of Peace.

ISAIAH 9:6 ESV

In the prophecies of Isaiah, he foretold the coming of Christ.
Jesus is our Wonderful Counselor, Mighty God, Everlasting
Father, and Prince of Peace. He is the long-awaited Savior
who takes away the sins of the world. He is our peace with
God, our everlasting King, and our wise and wonderful
Counselor in all things.

As you consider the first coming of Christ on this Christmas
Eve, meditate on the glory of God manifest in humanity. He
chose to come humbly. Though he dwelt with God from the
beginning in glory, he offered himself to put on the cloak of
flesh and bones, limiting his boundless essence to a body we
could recognize. What grace and mercy, true kindness and
love we can see and know in the person of Jesus Christ, our
wonderful God.

Everlasting God, thank you for the power of your choice
to become human in order to save humanity. You are
wonderful, and I am in awe of you.

JOYOUS TIDINGS

The angel said to them, "Do not be afraid, for behold, I bring you good tidings of great joy which will be to all people. For there is born to you this day in the city of David a Savior, who is Christ the Lord."

LUKE 2:10-11 NKJV

The birth of Jesus was good news for all. The Savior of the world was born. He who was from the beginning took on flesh and bones and came as a baby. He humbled himself to the human experience, being born in a stable to poor parents. From the start of his story, he related to the humble and offered hope to the weak.

He still does it today. Joyous tidings are ours in the coming of Christ. He came to set the captive free, heal the sick, and deliver the tormented. He brought peace with God as his gift to all. Let's worship him today with grateful hearts, for he is good to us. This joyous news of Christ's coming is our hope, and we hold to it, still, through every generation since his life, death, and resurrection.

Jesus, thank you for coming in the humblest of ways for the hope and salvation of all. I am awed by who you are.

KEEP GOING

We are surrounded by a great cloud of people
whose lives tell us what faith means.
So let us run the race that is before us
and never give up.

HEBREWS 12:1 NCV

When we grow tired on our own, we have only to remember that we are not alone in this race of life. We have those who have gone before, our heavenly cheer section, and those who are with us now to encourage our hearts in perseverance.

We each have a racecourse to run, and though the obstacles may be different for each of us, the finish line is the same. Let's look to those who lived with kingdom values as an encouragement to each of us to keep going: to stay the course and not give up. Whatever challenges we face, we are not alone in them. God is our help, and he offers us help through the encouragement, support, and faith of others. Let's not neglect the power of community in showing up and cheering each other on.

God, thank you for the power of witness, community, and encouragement. Where I am tempted to give up where you call me to keep pressing on, strengthen me in your mercy and in the power of supportive people. Thank you.

EVEN IF

"How could a loving mother forget her nursing child and not deeply love the one she bore? Even if there is a mother who forgets her child, I could never, no never, forget you."

ISAIAH 49:15 TPT

Those of us who are caregivers know the depth of love that moves us to care for our loved ones when they are helpless. Newborns are completely dependent on their parents to care for their needs. God reminds us of the power of a mother's love when he says, "But how could a loving mother forget her… child and not deeply love the one she bore?"

Not leaving anything to chance, God did not stop there. He said that even if there was a mother who could forget or neglect her child, that he would never, ever forget his children. You are God's child. In the family of Christ, you have a place in his kingdom. No one else can take it. God has not forgotten you, not even for a moment. You are before him in his thoughts. He deeply loves you and cares for you. Lean back into his loving arms, and rest in his affection today.

Loving Father, I am your child, and you are my Father. Reveal the depths of your loving heart toward me as I lean into your presence. I love you.

COMPLETELY CLEARED

[Love] keeps no record of wrongs.
1 CORINTHIANS 13:5 NIV

In our lives, we have many effects and consequences that we must deal with as a result of our choices. This is the way of the world. It is our human experience. When we are at fault, there are repercussions that filter from that. Even if we fail to take responsibility, the consequences still affect those around us.

When it comes to our relationship with the Lord, Christ's mercy covers every one of our missteps. There is nothing that can separate us from the love of God in Christ, not even our own sin. When we are liberated in the love of God, it is complete. When we walk in the love of God, we refuse to be easily irritated by little things and be slow in taking offense at others. In this way, we overlook offenses that don't harm others. When we don't nitpick at others' flaws, we are free to delight in who they are and what they offer, clearing them of our own judgment.

Lord, I know that accountability is necessary in your kingdom. Love does not avoid accountability, but it does also not look for reasons to hold grudges. Thank you for the wisdom and discernment you offer in love.

BEYOND MEASURE

We know how much God loves us,
and we have put our trust in his love.
God is love, and all who live in love live in God,
and God lives in them.

1 JOHN 4:16 NLT

God is love. With his very being, with all that he is, God loves us. If God cannot be measured, neither can his love. His power emanates from the essence of his mercy-kindness. Everything, then, finds its source in love from the very beginning.

When we live in love, we live in God. God lives in us. Why would we seek to limit our expressions of love when it is the very limitless of God's kindness that reaches each of us and folds us into the kingdom of God? We can grow in love every day, seeking new ways to express the kindness of God in action. We can step outside the comfort of what feels possible into the realm of the impossible as we partner with God's love in our lives and communities. We have only just tasted and seen; let's keep going until we're feasting on his goodness through lived-out mercy-kindness.

Source of Love, thank you for creating me, my neighbors, and this world in your image: in love's image. I want to grow in living out your love every day. Show me ways I can practically show kindness and live it out well.

COMING OR GOING

The LORD will protect you from all evil;
he will keep your soul.
The LORD will guard your going out and your coming in
from this time and forever.

PSALM 121:7-8 NASB

When you leave your home and when you safely return, God himself guards you. He watches over you and keeps you safe. No matter what this coming year holds, God goes with you. He steps into the areas that are completely unknown to you as you move. He is aware of all the cracks and traps, as well as the gifts and victories that await you.

Trust him to lead you, and to lead you well. He is full of wisdom, faithfulness, and peace. He has all that you need for every step of your journey. And when you return to places and spaces you have not been in a while, he goes with you then, too. He is with you, and he will guard you, whether you're going out or returning.

Wise God, I trust you to guard me in goodness and to lead me in kindness, no matter where I go. May your peace be my plentiful portion every step of my journey. Thank you.

A BRIGHT HOPE

"Look, God's dwelling is with humanity, and he will live with them. They will be his peoples, and God himself will be with them and will be their God. He will wipe away every tear from their eyes. Death will be no more; grief, crying, and pain will be no more, because the previous things have passed away."

REVELATION 21:3-4 CSB

No matter what this past year has brought you through or where this next year may take you, God is faithful to his promises. He will not leave you, not even for a moment. Beyond the scope of this one, short life, lies a greater hope: that we will dwell with Christ in his kingdom. In this place, beautiful and hopeful, he will wipe every tear from our eyes.

When we go through seasons of suffering, let's remember what Paul said in 2 Corinthians 4:17: "For this slight momentary affliction is preparing us for an eternal weight of glory beyond all measure." In that place, death will be no more; mourning and crying and pain will be no more. Those things will have passed away. So let's hold onto our bright and burning hope. Jesus is with us, and he is guiding us into the fullness of his kingdom with every step of our journey.

My God, I have hope that suffering will not last forever. I believe there is so much goodness ahead. I trust you, my living and faithful hope.